THE IRON MAN
IN INDUSTRY

AN OUTLINE
OF THE SOCIAL SIGNIFICANCE
OF
AUTOMATIC MACHINERY

BY
ARTHUR POUND

BOSTON
THE ATLANTIC MONTHLY PRESS

Printed in United States of America

This book is inscribed to the memory of

WILLIAM A. PATERSON
1838 — 1921

In his youth a master craftsman at the
forge, and for more than half a century
an employer who kept faith with his
men, his market, and his community.

PREFACE

IT has been my luck, for twenty years, to work in factory towns at a trade which kept both mind and office open to all comers. I have been employer and employed, reporter, editor, and printer, proprietor, partner and shareholder of and in various enterprises, most of them concerned with spreading news and views. With enough experience of business, if assimilated in the usual way, to have made me a business man, I remain a newspaper man. Business men must be specialists; newspaper men ought to be generalists.

Libraries are full of books on industrial problems, which I have not had time to read; but there is no type of man in industry that I have not met and heard through to the end of his string. Such slight researches as I have made, however, indicate that the favored styles in books on industry are two: the coldly analytical and the hotly polemical. The results prove that, in books, life may be analyzed into lifelessness and beaten to death with verbal lashes, while outside their covers life and work push on regardless. So it seemed worth while to attempt a discussion of the industrial problem which should be neither hot rhetoric nor cold analysis, but rather a calm synthesis, — calm yet not altogether devoid of warmth, — and so far new as to take into account impacts of new tools and methods upon human nature and the social order.

Large numbers of persons, most of them unwittingly, have assisted me in this work through the conversations of many talkative years. I am most grateful, however, to Mr. Ernest F. Lloyd, of Ann Arbor, Michigan, a former manufacturer of gas-machinery and operator of gas companies, who, after a busy life, retired to the academic atmosphere of a college town, to reflect upon his experience. Entering the University as a special student in economics when past middle age, he reversed, with most interesting results, the educational process. His forthcoming book on "The Wages System" is the clearest analyis yet made of our industrial system as it operates; and I joyfully advertise his priority of thought in many conclusions reached in this volume. Those chapters which stress the economic aspect are, in effect, the fruits of joint authorship; and throughout I have had the benefit of his accurate knowledge of industry and his firm grip on economic theory. Without his aid this book scarcely could have been written, though I make haste to absolve him from responsibility of agreement in all its conclusions, since we have our individual points of view on many of the issues.

My thanks are likewise due to Dr. C. B. Burr, author of "Practical Psychology and Psychiatry," for expert advice and steady encouragement; to Dr. G. K. Pratt of the Massachusetts Society for Mental Hygiene, and to Dr. Arnold L. Jacoby, psychiatrist of the Municipal Courts of Detroit, for assistance in endeavoring to untangle the mental threads of the complex.

ARTHUR POUND.

CONTENTS

Page

INTRODUCTION

I FROM LAND TO MILL 1

II THE LEVELING OF WAGES 18

III MIND AND MACHINE 36

IV THE IRON DUKES 62

V INDUSTRY AND THE STATE 87

VI THE CHANGING CORPORATION . . . 114

VII THE JOB AND SOCIETY 141

VIII WAR AND WORK 153

IX THE IRON MAN'S LEGACY 170

X EDUCATION FOR LEISURE 196

XI GOD AND MAN 216

INTRODUCTION

IN the pastoral age, affirms the poet Tagore, man explored space, and exploited it through the media of his nibbling beasts. Through agriculture he explored time, laboriously binding the seasons to his purposes. There Eastern civilization remains to-day, having added, of its own free will, only the handicrafts, though slave power permitted such enormous extension of hand-processes that many of its public works remain notable for size as well as detail. But the Western peoples, more ambitious and less contemplative, crept out of agriculture and the handicrafts by harnessing natural forces, and building machines that multiplied man-power. They wedded science to toil, and system to acquisitiveness. They educated other peoples, as well as themselves, in wants; organized international exchanges of goods and services; policed the high seas; and swept on to the political hegemony of the planet.

As the beast was the essential of pastoral life, and the tool the essential of agricultural life, so the machine is the essential of the industrial civilization in which we dwell. We tend our flocks of machines as zealously as Abraham's servants tended his herds, and for the same reason — because they are the means of existence. We ply our reapers to the same end that Cain plied his sickle. Our cranes, lathes, and steamshovels are to us precisely what the lever was to the builder, the chisel to the shaper of stone and metal, and the spade to the villein, in the centuries between Solomon and Napoleon — means of reducing matter to the use and comfort of man.

Machine-mounted, we tilt furiously at time and space. A chase foredoomed to failure, say the philosophers. So be it; yet, except at rare intervals, we heed these croakers little, each generation confident, almost to the grave, that through speed and quantity man shall yet break through to the millennium. But no matter how swiftly our inventors improve our steel steed, somehow we never succeed in lessening perceptibly the distance to that far horizon.

At times, in spite of warning signals, we come croppers that invite despair,—as in 1914. In such situations we gaze panic-stricken upon the wreckage of humanity and the wastage of its heritage through all the ages. But we are of breeds not easily cast down, breeds avid of power and conscious of high destinies. So, after agreeing that we must have come the wrong road, we reconnoitre the ground, only to develop the uncomfortable truth that we cannot go back. There is too much débris, of our own making, behind us, to permit retreat. Scouts, self-appointed but desperately in earnest, bring in word of glimpses of fair and level roads to right or left — the Radicals saying left, and the Conservatives right; but most of us conclude that the intervening jungle presents insuperable obstacles to any drastic change in civilization's right of way.

Above the turmoil, the drivers and mechanicians lift voices to command or implore. "A few light repairs," they say, "and we will soon have the old machine under way again, practically as good as new, providing labor takes hold with a will. Lay to, men!" But labor mutters and draws back.

Others insist that the thing to do is to improve the road — from this point, on to infinity. Still others declare that it is time to lighten cargo, to throw overboard age-honored and hard-won possessions, traditions, customs, conventions, laws — the baggage of society.

In all this agitated company there remain but few who, bearing no grudges and offering no panaceas, seek the outskirts of the milling throng. There, by ones and twos, ignoring importunities to get busy, they reflect upon the complex "why" of the catastrophe; and consider what more is likely to happen if the same pilots push the same machine ahead, at the old, heart-breaking pace, heedless of the degenerating effect of jolt and friction upon its fine-wrought parts and upon the even more delicate minds and bodies, faiths and loyalties, of their myriad fellow passengers. And what of those frail but indispensable fibres of human confidence and sympathy, which bind individuals into groups, inducing a cohesion whereby those groups may realize something of their common yearnings in institutions — in homes, schools, churches, associations, corporations, unions, societies, and states.

In short, civilization has had a desperate mauling.

Certain forces and mechanisms, brought into the House of Life as servants, have usurped undue authority, on the flashy but insufficient warrant of the wealth they produce. It is time to show them their places and keep them there.

THE IRON MAN
IN INDUSTRY

I

FROM LAND TO MILL

FIRST, the man and the beast; then, the man and the hand-tool; now, the man and the machine-tool!

This is the century of the automatic machine. The social problem is to accommodate the use of automatic machinery to the well-being of the masses; our political problem is to avert class and state wars growing out of quarrels over the profits, powers, and privileges accruing through the production and marketing of goods. Much of our modern heart-searching, if intelligently directed, leads down to the Iron Man at the base of the industrial structure. He claims the twentieth century as his; the social and economic forces that he releases are those most likely to carry on into the future the reality of our day.

"Machine-tools may be classified in two main groups: those which lengthen and strengthen the arm of the worker without displacing his will as the vital function of work, and those whose principal function is to supplant the worker, or to reduce his function to a minimum." (Lloyd)

An example of the first class is the jib crane. The operator must direct the machine; his mind must work with his muscle precisely as his forbears had to apply both mind and muscle to their simple levers.

In the second class, the ability to do the work is a primary function of the machine itself, and inherent in the mechanism. Designed to accomplish its task independent of human direction, the attendant need not know the necessary steps that the machine takes in doing the work. He need not know how to repair it in case of a jam: that is another man's job. All the attendant is required to do is to feed the machine with material and relieve it of produce. Even starting and stopping the machine may be done by another, so minutely is the work-function divided.

Of course, there are varying degrees of completeness in the application of the self-functioning principle to machinery. Some machines are nearly automatic. The pneumatic riveter, for instance, requires skill for its operation, but the technique is more easily attained than that of the hand-riveter. However, the trend toward complete automatization is strong and steady throughout industry.

I have witnessed, recently, the premier of a completely automatic machine in a branch of production which, fifteen years ago, was prosecuted almost entirely by hand. This automatic cost upwards of $30,000 to install, supplanting a semi-automatic machine, which called for the exercise of two distinct acts of judgment on the part of its attendant. Frequent bungling of these two operations spoiled so much material that the new machine is considered a marked advance. The attendant now is practically without other responsibility than that of inserting the material and withdrawing the product.

This illustrates the steady progress toward automatization, a progress dictated by economic considerations of the first magnitude, and certain to continue until the highest possible application of the automatic principle has been reached. The flour mills of Minneapolis and Kansas City are probably our best examples of automatic production, the wheat being milled, measured, and packed for shipment by machinery so comprehensive that very few operatives are required; and as a result, the milling industry has no bothersome labor problem.

The principle of automatic functioning in machinery is almost as old as machinery itself; but its common application is comparatively recent — so recent that the beginning of the twentieth century may be considered a turning-point. As a determining factor in modern industry, it dates from the late eighties, when the moulding machine first appeared in American foundries. In this machine the automatic principle, which hitherto had been more or less casually applied, found an abiding-place. Its potency seems not to have been generally recognized; but employers found in it an aid to strike-breaking. With its assistance, an unskilled laborer, after short training, on certain kinds of work could equal the best efforts of the old-time moulder. The new device threw down the gage of battle to organized labor in one of its most

completely organized fields. No one saw in it the
herald of an industrial revolution, or discerned in its
operations the beginnings of a new evolutionary force
in social relations. Through the nineties the moulding machine fought its way against the conservatism
of employers and the opposition of union labor. By
1900, it had reached a highly improved form, capable
of making an enlarged variety of articles of intricate
and complex patterns.

This practical testimony to the validity of the
automatic principle in production encouraged its
application to complementary trades. Inventive
America quickly produced the turret lathe, the screw
machine, the pneumatic hammer, the grinding machine, and scores of other devices designed to multiply
man-power and reduce the individual operative's
responsibility for the quality of the finished product.
As skill became less and less essential, the apprenticeship system died a natural death. Factories were
opened to unskilled workers. At the same time, the
quantity of output per worker increased, and its
quality improved. The Iron Man, having no nerves,
and being created for a single purpose, did "repeat"
work better than trained men. Production increased
rapidly; the power of man to satisfy his expanding
wants leaped ahead. This increase marked one of
those abrupt turns on the road of industry which
impart to civilization a new direction.

It is noteworthy that the general acceptance and
rapid development of automatic machinery coincided
with the acceptance and development of the automo-

bile. As a commodity, the automobile was accepted by the public almost overnight; as a human want, it burst into being rather than grew. Moreover, the automobile was not a development of an existing method of transportation, but was in itself a new means of transportation. Its manufacturers, consequently, faced their all-demanding market with open minds. They had little or nothing to junk in order to install the latest machines; the rewards of enterprise were so great that the best automatic machinery quickly paid for itself and produced profits. Quantity production, standardization of parts, extreme accuracy—these ensured wide scope for automatic machinery in automobile production.

The war, with its insistent demand for quantity and its terrible drain upon labor-power, immensely stimulated the development of the Iron Man. Shifting the industrial function from the man to the machine produced, and is still producing, corresponding shifts in other fields of action. The balance of economic power was disturbed, with consequent notable reactions upon society, precisely as the political structure of the globe shakes whenever the economic balance of power is upset.

Perhaps the most apparent of these reactions was the unsettling of the ratio of population between city and country. The slogan "Back to the Land" is about twenty years old. By 1905 the chorus grew so loud, that President Roosevelt appointed a Country-Life Commission, to formulate a programme for keeping people on the farms. Its exhaustive report had little effect: cities continued growing at the expense of the countryside. The 1910 census verified alarmist predictions; nevertheless, in spite of agitation, the current grew in breadth and speed, until by 1920 it had become a flood. For the first time in American history, January, 1920, saw more than half the people of the United States living in cities and villages of more than 2500 population.

By chance, the 1920 census was taken at the peak of the flood, and represents a high-water mark of urban congestion. The situation suddenly reversed itself. In midsummer of 1920, people began to leave town. Practically all cities dependent upon industry lost in population. As might have been expected, those which had grown most rapidly lost most rapidly, since, with man as with nature, quick growth means weak roots. Perhaps the heaviest losses were sustained by cities equipped for automobile production. The trend of population now sets unmistakably toward the rural districts.

Why this sudden shift? What counter-force, suddenly applied, sufficed to check so quickly a force operative for twenty years, and so powerful that it defied the denouncements of articulate public opinion? There is nothing subtle or hidden about that counter-force. Economic advantage brought country-folk to town, and now takes them back to the land. They came cityward for jobs, stayed as long as the jobs lasted, and turned landward when the jobs failed. They came to operate, or rather to tend, automatic machinery. When that machinery, with their assist-

ance, glutted the market for the time being, as many
of the operatives as could make the change advantageously cut back toward the old homestead and the
familiar rural scene. While the city of Detroit was
losing approximately 200,000 in population in six
months (part of which has since been regained),
Michigan villages have been growing. While Flint,
Michigan, lost 15,000, the village of Montrose, eighteen miles away, gained one hundred, or 20 per cent of
its census enumeration. Two thousand persons are
reported to have left Akron, Ohio, in a single day,
heading back toward locations where work on the
land is the chief pursuit of man.

The Michigan Congregational Conference reviewed
the situation which presented itself to rural pastors
when the "prodigal sons, without jobs or funds,"
returned to the rural districts in droves. The return
was not as pleasant as the going; the economic pull
toward good fortune is far easier on human nature
than the economic push away from short rations.
They went in hope, and returned disillusioned.
Nevertheless, they did return, thereby relieving the
crowded housing conditions of manufacturing towns,
and filling with labor-power many crevices and hol-
lows in the vast, and of late undermanned, field of
rural economy. They will return to town if and when
wanted. The Iron Man of Industry beckoned them
to town; the market glut created by multiplication
of man-power drove them back to the villages and
farms; and the Iron Man will bring them back when
real factory-wages temporarily rise above real farm-

wages. By removing the ancient obstruction in the pipe-line connecting town and rural labor-supplies, the automatic tool wrought a channel for free labor-flow between town and country.

Let us examine more closely the manner in which the automatic tool forced this leveling of labor. In 1901, the International Order of Machinists called a nation-wide strike. Through strict control of the apprentice system, the machinists had limited their numbers rigidly. As the aristocrats of the labor world, enjoying top wages, they were well financed for the struggle. That strike was one of the decisive battles of industrial history; its stake, although scarcely realized at the time, was control of the conditions under which automatic machines would be operated, which, in turn, would have meant control of America's future.

The strikers lost; from that blow union labor never fully recovered. Thenceforth the growth of the open shop was sure as fate. The strikers lost, because enough automatic machinery had been installed to produce essential supplies, and because employers not so equipped saw that by installing the new tools they could carry on with less dependence upon skilled help. Immediately industries of all sorts entered the market for automatic machinery. The demand, so fanned, brought forth a steady stream of inventions and improvements, which, continuing to this day, has created a new set of industrial relationships, with all manner of direct and indirect effects upon social and political institutions. America, since 1905, has marched to the staccato tune of the automatic tool.

Immediately, the factories began to draw upon the countryside for labor. Toward the beginning of the century, the rural districts possessed a surplus population accumulated during the preceding decade. Country birth-rates are usually higher than city birth-rates, and rural death-rates lower than city death-rates. It is an axiom that the country produces population, and the cities consume population. From 1800, the surplus farm-population had been drained steadily away from its points of origin by the opening of the West. American farm-folk, aided and abetted by immigrant farmers, pushed the frontier steadily from the Alleghanies to the Pacific. These pioneers found fertile land, much of it almost ready-made for farming and requiring little capital to fit it for extensive agriculture. By 1890, however, only the inferior spots and less accessible areas of the once vast public domain remained open to homesteaders. These leavings required more capital per acre before they could be worked profitably. The day had passed when the young farmer could make good on a homestead through his own labor and the small financial assistance to be counted upon from home. Consequently, westward migration slowed down; the new crop of country boys and girls stayed closer to home; gradually, surplus population appeared in the rural districts. This slowing down of the westward migration contributed greatly to the "hard times" of the early nineties. Then, as now, a depressed agriculture means a depressed nation, economically.

Do not infer that the surplus rural population so created was unemployed. Rather, it was underemployed, not utilized to full advantage. Its members worked steadily as long as there was work to do. They earned their livings; little more. Wages were low; employment, seasonal; existence, practically on the subsistence basis. For the married farm-hand or woodsman there was no chance to get ahead except by grinding thrift and low-standard living. Farm tenants and small-farm owners were little better off, and Populism flourished as a natural result.

This growing labor-surplus acted as a check upon farm-machinery sales. Man-power on the farm became so cheap that farm-implement makers feared that improved machines might not be salable. When the West was being brought under control by the American farmer, he needed machines to multiply man-power; and those he left behind needed machinery to make up for his absence. Demand brought forth improved farm machines, in such abundance and of such economic effects, that it is not stretching the truth to say that without them Europe's industrial development could not have reached its antewar proportions.

In this sense Cyrus McCormick,— or whoever it was that invented the reaper, McCormick's priority being questioned,— was one of the real founders of modern Germany. Except for cheap food produced with machine assistance, the industrial cities of

Western Europe could not have attained their present size.

However, the situation that brought forth these improved farm machines had changed considerably by the nineties. The farmer, with grown sons and daughters to feed, faced the problem of keeping them economically employed. He was not likely to buy a machine that would throw his own flesh and blood out of work, unless the lad, or girl, could go elsewhere and support himself. Consequently, manufacturers of farm machinery, competing against cheap labor and family loyalty, concluded to standardize their lines. The future, they believed, called for every possible economy of manufacture and distribution, even to the point of possible monopoly control of the market. They began to merge plants; to coöperate instead of compete. The year 1902 saw the International Harvester Company — the giant in its field — organized, after negotiations covering several years. It is possible, of course, to interpret such mergers as brazen assaults on the public purse; but in this case, it seems to have been rather a case of manufacturers running to cover in common cyclone-cellars, before the storm-cloud of threatening conditions for their particular industry. Little did these manufacturers guess that the automatic tool was about to relieve their machines of cheap-labor competition, and in a few years produce such a shortage of rural labor that every improvement in farm machinery would become immediately salable.

Farm laborers, in this plight, turned longing eyes

toward the towns and cities. Against all obstacles the
country has persisted in feeding the cities, not alone
with food, but also with youth. At this juncture,
however, the urban prospect was about as bad for the
country boy as it had ever been. He was expected
to remain, and usually did remain, on the place
as a boy-helper without wages, until he reached his
majority. If he turned to town at from twenty-one
to twenty-five, he found the ranks of casual labor
overcrowded. Unless he went through an apprenticeship of several years, his only chance to get into a
factory was as a roustabout. Skill, born of training
and ꞏexperience, dominated the situation; trained
mechanics held the good jobs; their sons filled the
apprentice-rolls. If the farm youth entered apprenticeship, he worked alongside boys much younger
than himself, who lived at home and contributed
their small earnings to the family welfare, even as he
had done. His apprentice wage would be only a
fraction of what he could earn, by strength alone, at
unskilled labor. Of course, some farm boys per-
severed against this handicap, and rose to become
sound mechanics, and even heads of industrial enterprises. Others were indentured early by farsighted
parents. But we are dealing with mass effects. In
general, conditions inherent in the differing economies
of farm and factory conspired to seal factory gates
against farm boys.

This was the situation when automatic machinery
began to be applied in quantity to industrial pro-

duction — a turning-point which may be roughly considered as coincident with the opening of the twentieth century. The first effect of the automatic tool was to deal the apprentice system a death-blow. It lingers on in many trades, but is no longer a determining factor in the basic industries, because automatic machinery has forced factory gates ajar for all men of ordinary intelligence and average manual dexterity. Gradually, but in increasing volume, the surplus labor of the countryside, whose power was not being fully exploited on the land, began to flow toward higher wages and the comforts and amusements to be purchased with those wages.

The flow slowed down somewhat in 1913, when industry marked time appreciably, indicating that production had outrun consumption. By the latter year industry had drawn off the surplus farm population; and it might have rested there, content with the farm youth. But, at the close of 1914, with enormous war-profits in the offing, and heavy orders from Europe showing that the war-torn Continent would pay well for the produce of American machines, industry reached out for the farm men. By overbidding rural employers, the mills got their men in such numbers that the industrial cities could not house them and their families. Farm-wages and prices, gradually rising all through this transition, now leaped upward; but not fast enough to prevent farms from being abandoned.

The post-war period of industrial expansion, on the shaky base of inflated currency and credits, brought the townward movement to its apogee. In Michigan, where the common use of automatic machinery in automobile production had forced a larger percentage of urban growth than in any state in the Union, the authorities, in the spring of 1920, reported 30,000 vacant farm and village dwellings, at the same time that every industrial city in the state was wrestling with the problem of housing its new-won population. But the moment sound finance called the turn on inflation and expansion, economic necessity swung the human tide back toward the countryside.

Still another large class of workers, designated, perhaps unjustly, as unskilled, found economic release from low wages through the introduction of automatic machinery. These were women domestic servants. Housework, until quite recently, was the chief economic refuge of untrained women without means. Some city girls went into stores and offices, laundries, and light manufacturing, particularly textiles and clothing; but the other important factory-industries had remained more or less closed to women. Women never would have entered upon apprentice-ships in large numbers, even if freely admitted; for the good reason that most women at the apprentice age are looking forward to marriage and housekeeping, in which occupation specialized trade skill is largely wasted. Domestic service, in fact, is better training for wifehood than any mill occupation.

These considerations kept the ranks full in spite of low wages. Moreover, in the rural offing, there were always plenty of "hired girls" ready to come into town — the sisters of the farm boys whose economic progress has been already noted. They were encouraged to come, because one less mouth to feed left more for the others. At the close of the century, it was not even economical to use these girls on the land, because male labor was so abundant and cheap. When male help became scarce enough to make women's coöperation in the active outdoor work of the farm profitable, farmers' daughters began to don overalls and produce crops. Not chivalry, but economics, had dictated their previous immunity from field labor; our prejudice against such work did not stand the economic test.

However, automatic machinery opened factory gates to women as well as men. Since men were preferred for most factory jobs, by reason of their greater occupational permanence and resistance to fatigue, domestic servants entered industry less rapidly than did the farm males. Some of them found their way gradually into industry before 1914; but the great feminist drive upon machines did not start in earnest until the war reduced the man-power available for machine labor. Then the home women, with a solidarity that could hardly have been improved upon by organization, left house-service for the mills. In a few months domestic-service-wages leaped to a parity with real mill-wages, as farm-wages had done previously over a longer period. When the hand that tends the range can tend the lathe as well, why take less for one job than for the other?

But no sooner had the factories begun to slow

down, than domestic servants became more plentiful. Like the boys from the farms, some of the women are going back to housework, disillusioned, fed up on factory employment, with its haste, nerve-strain, and insecurity of tenure. But they are in the minority, and do not affect the general proposition, that the automatic tool has brought the home and the mill into direct competition for labor.

What does all this mean for the future of America? History — even recent history — means little to America except as a basis from which to project the future. As a people, we prefer looking forward rather than back. This force, which has worked so powerfully upon us, leveling wages, shifting population, determining home-sites and living conditions, is still in its infancy. Presumably it must continue its power into the future, leaving no department of life unmoved by its impact. What, in short, are likely to be the effects of the common and growing use of automatic machinery in industrial production upon American life, political institutions, and social standards, upon homes, schools, and children?

This is an inquiry as broad in scope as humanity itself, and cutting down to the roots of life. And it is so complicated that, in projecting the view, we must be content with citing tendencies and making due allowances for unknown quantities in the equation, even at the risk of vagueness. But the essential importance of the inquiry cannot be overestimated. If we catch, even hazily, some idea of what reasonably may be expected, we are not likely to be shocked into combating the inevitable; but, instead, shall accommodate ourselves to it like sensible beings. Since the automatic tool works upon human nature as directly as it works upon materials, which physical action trained minds forecast accurately, qualified intelligences should be able to forecast, at least in part, the economic, social, and political effects of the same machinery. By no other method can we come upon the path to the rational evolution of industrial society; certainly we shall never find it by idle drifting or hateful smashing of our institutional birthrights. To focus the attention of clear and open minds upon this new reagent in the social equation — the Iron Man in Industry — is the object of this book.

II

THE LEVELING OF WAGES

OPERATING an automatic machine requires no more than average manual dexterity and ordinary intelligence. In some cases, where the materials in process are heavy, it requires considerable strength and, where several machines are grouped in one man's care, considerable agility. If the operative is willing to trust the company to figure his pay without checking up in his own interest, no book knowledge is necessary. Simple arithmetic and ability to sign one's name are the top intellectual requirements. Most manufacturers, however, prefer to have their employees read, write, and understand English, though this knowledge is by no means necessary. Consequently, many companies provide instruction in English for immigrants. In general, the ordinary public-school instruction, up to and including the eighth grade, gives a youth all the mental furnishing he needs to function efficiently in automatic production. Considered strictly as an economic being, he could get along with less. When we come to the salaried workers, the so-called white-collar group, we find public education reinforcing the leveling tendency in those branches, just as automatic machinery does in the mills.

Thus far we have considered the automatic machine leveling wages and distributing labor as between the farm and factory, home and mill. In much the same way, the spreading use of automatic machinery tends to level wages in all plants so equipped, though hindered at many points by special conditions and special labor contracts. Certain automatic machines are widely scattered, and can be found in every industrial centre. Many others present family likenesses. Even the greenest of green workers needs but short tutelage at his assigned machine; while the man who knows how much — or rather how little — is expected of him, can shake down quickly into efficient production. The per-capita cost of labor turnover on the 1920 basis of pay ranged from $25 to $100 per man in the more efficiently organized automobile plants, this cost including the pay of the novice and his teacher, the overhead on machine, and allowance for spoiled work. This verifies the evidence presented by a survey of certain large allied plants, to the effect that 70 per cent of the employees could be fitted into their jobs in three days or less. This means that a worker can shift from one line of production to another without grave loss of time. He may be a woodcutter or harvest hand this month, and a producer of automobile parts the next. If of a roving disposition, in a single year he may can salmon on the Pacific Coast, pour cement on an irrigation dam in Idaho, mill flour in Minnesota, cut pearl buttons in Iowa, mould iron in Ohio, weave silk in Jersey, and make rubber tires in New England. If this is not an exact statement at this writing, it is fast coming true, as skill is more and more transferred from man to machine. The outcome of such easy transitions must be a highly efficient distribution of labor-power on the one hand, and, on the other, a progressive leveling of wages as among all automatized industries. "The old trade-demarcations," says Lloyd, "have largely ceased to exist; and with their passing the old differences of pay have correspondingly declined."

This leveling tendency, moreover, is no respecter of sex. Since women can tend many automatic tools as well as men, it follows that the wages of the two sexes must draw together. They may never reach uniformity, because many women view jobs as temporary stop-gaps on the road to marriage, and this handicaps them as yet in the eyes of many employers. This, and kindred non-economic considerations, may affect the result; but they cannot stop the drift toward equality of wage. It is no unusual thing, even now, to find a young wife earning as much as, or more than, her husband. As time goes on, this will become too common to command notice.

Likewise, automatic machinery tends to break down the former disparity of wage as between age and youth. Children of twelve can tend many automatic machines as competently as adults. Youths, in fact, approach their highest wage during the very years in which the boys of a generation ago were earning less than living wages as apprentices. Eighteen to twenty-five are the most gainful years for the "machinate mammal."

The leveling proceeds with ruthless disregard for race or nationality. While a knowledge of the native tongue may be desirable, it is by no means essential.

Witness the widespread employment of our newly arrived immigrants on automatic machines, their earnings on a par with those of native-born products of our public schools. Notwithstanding that the color-line rarely gives the negro a chance at automatics, the black populations of our northern industrial cities increased faster than the white populations from 1910 to 1920. Bringing black labor north became a highly organized enterprise. The pay for negroes, generally speaking, maintained a parity with white labor on the same kind of work; and while blacks are not often put on machines, there is no doubt that many blacks can fill the requirements of machine attendance. Whether they can stand the steady grind as well as whites, or whether the color-line is justifiably drawn at the machine, are moot points, reserved for future discussion. But the general effect of the automatizing process has been to bring the average wages of the two races closer together, not only in the industrial cities, but, to an even greater extent, in those sections where the black does most of the field-work. Increased cotton-picking costs and increased wheat-growing costs both resulted from the drain which automatic production put upon rural labor-supplies.

Automatic machines in offices affect the "white-collar" group in industry precisely as shop-workers are affected. With adding machines and other mechanisms, and standardized office-systems, need for special skill is decreasing among office-workers. The old-fashioned bookkeeper, the aristocrat of *fin-de-siècle* offices, is fast becoming as obsolete a type as the old-fashioned mechanic, the one-time aristocrat of the shops. Stenographic skill is subject to the competition of the phonograph; the typist is entering into competition with the duplicating typewriter. Meanwhile, public schools and business colleges are producing an abundance of persons sufficiently educated for the simplified office tasks. In addition, the higher social status enjoyed by such workers can be depended upon to furnish surplus labor for such activities in ordinary times; with the result that we pay practically the same rate to washerwomen and typists; also to cooks and stenographers, when board-and-lodging costs are considered. These influences tended to bring office-work down to the wage-level of factory-work before the war; as office-workers began to go over into the ranks of factory-workers, owing to war-wage rates in the factories, office-wages began to rise. From this time on, owing to the fact that labor can flow from one group to the other more easily than ever before, disparity of wage between the two groups will tend to correct itself promptly.

Transferring the vital function of production from the operative to the machine involves taking a certain skill away from the rank and file and concentrating it in the directing and organizing end of industry. The heats of competition, playing through machine improvements, evaporate skill from the lower reaches of industry and distill it in the upper reaches. Fewer producers need skill; but those few require much longer training and more highly intensified mental powers. It is up to them, not only to design, build, place, and adapt machines to involved tasks, but also to work out systems under which the production of those machines can be coördinated and the produce distributed.

To fit an automatic machine for its production-cycle requires high skill in tool-designing and pattern-making. Head and hand must work together; jigs and dies must be of the utmost precision. The number of skilled workmen required for this task is small compared to the whole number of industrial employees; but the group is of key importance. In the past, these men were trained under the apprentice system; but that system being in decline, industrial executives are greatly concerned for the future supply of such craftsmen. They look to public education to guard against a famine of skilled artisans; and such is their influence, that they are not likely to look in vain. The call of industry has been answered already by the establishment of technical high-schools and colleges in many industrial cities, as well as by the erection of private trade-schools. In desperation some employers have established their own trade-schools; but the outlook is that public education, thus challenged, will take up the burden of providing industry with skilled mechanics. Once adequate facilities are provided, we may look with assurance for the greater mental interest attaching to that work to provide candidates in abundance, and so increase the number of qualified men to the point where the pay shall approach that of the machine-tender — always being enough more, presumably,

to make up for the time and cost of training.
The next layer in the skill compartment contains
technical experts, shop-organizers, and salesmen. The
third layer includes the executives. It is in these
two layers that the thought-processes of modern industry centre; and the demands for special knowledge
are such that their personnel must be far better
equipped than their predecessors in the old régime.
In the swift expansion of automatized industry they
have been forced further and further afield, for labor
and materials on the one hand, and for markets on
the other hand. They have been required to finance,
not only the inflow of men and machines, but also
the outflow of goods — a task so vast and compelling
that it has brought into being a distinct adaptation
of the banking function to industrial needs.

In a very real sense, bankers are the aristocrats of
modern industry — sitting apart from the actual
processes of production and distribution, but furnishing the lifeblood of capital, and through that power
exercising a genuine, and usually salutary, control.
How are these thought-men of industry going to be
affected by these leveling forces at work in modern
society? Are they going to be leveled economically
by the same forces that brought them such large
rewards? Of late years, in the era of industrial expansion, they have commanded large salaries. What
is likely to happen to them now that the wheels of
industry are slowing down?

So far as the technical experts — chiefly chemists
and engineers — are concerned, the situation is fairly

clear. They are being turned out in such numbers by colleges and universities that, except in sudden bursts of industrial expansion, the supply tends to outrun the demand. There is no wide rift between the pay of a Bachelor of Science, just out of college, and the pay of a factory operative. A city-engineering department can hire draughtsmen about as cheaply as common laborers. All institutions of higher learning are growing in attendance, particularly in the technical branches. Also, the training tends to become more thorough, hence more productive of men fitted to move in the highest circles of industrial production. From all indications, universities and colleges are as apt to flood the market with engineers and chemists as the mothers of the country are to flood it with unskilled labor. Public education, therefore, tends to level toward the general average the pay for such service.

Salesmanship is similarly affected. The personal element does not play the large part that it once played in disposing of goods. The influence of advertising is to create a market condition in which the salesman becomes more and more of an "order-taker," disposing of standardized, guaranteed goods at prices and on terms set by his superiors in the organization. As dickering is thrust out of the sales-equation, the personal shrewdness of the salesman counts for less and less. His efficiency comes to depend less upon native traits and more upon what can be taught him. Salesmen of the old school were born, not made; but salesmen of the new school can be made out of any

normally aggressive public-school product. Schools
for salesmanship, established here and there, are
likely to succeed. In general, the process of distributing goods tends to become more scientific and less
personal; and, as that change proceeds, the humbler
members of the sales-organization become less important, and more candidates are available. The net
result is that the salesman's wage tends toward the
common wage-level. The retail sales-clerk, male or
female, earns no more than he or she could earn in a
factory.

The small retail grocer, whose chief function is that
of taking orders, complains because he is being run
out of business by a chain store, whose manager is
frankly an order-taker, and earns, usually, no more
than the average wage of the community. His employer, safeguarded by the cash register and an office-
system imposing a close check, finds it unnecessary
to pay a bonus for character and honesty. The
traveling salesman is not the bold, free man of other
days; he covers more territory than the "drummer"
of twenty years ago, but he does not have equal responsibility. The tendency, all along the line, is for
salesmen's wages to keep in closer touch with the
wage-level in the producing end of the business.

The situation as respects employers is even more
difficult to analyze, because executive ability is so
largely applied native force, energy, will-power. Executives, up to date, have been largely self-trained.
However, of late, the universities and colleges, recognizing that industrial executives are the most power-

ful figures in an industrial civilization, have taken steps to train men for these posts. Hence their schools of finance and commerce; hence their courses in business practice; hence the announcements that the universities must train "for life."

If the educational system makes good on this programme, it is evident that executive salaries must fall. They have always been higher here than abroad. Foreign managers are content with less pay and more prestige. Already the trend is downward. In practically every industrial receivership, the receiver's first step has been to reduce executive salaries. This leveling-down is matched by an equally significant recent leveling-up in the salaries of minor executives, who were left behind in the war raises for the rank and file, by means of which the laborer, in many cases, came to earn more than the man from whom he took his orders directly. The Pennsylvania Railroad, for example, some months ago raised all its operating officials up to the grade of superintendent, while the higher executives were not raised.

Consideration of executive salaries, from this standpoint of wage-leveling, is complicated by the fact that many executives play a dual rôle in industry. They are heavy stockholders as well as managers of other persons' capital. Some managers, in fact, own majority interests in the corporations they captain; the corporation, then, is actually the lengthened shadow of the man — and none too lengthened, at that. In such cases, managers draw as salaries part of the profits which otherwise would be apportioned as dividends, since competition for leadership does not enter into the equation. This practice has been accelerated by the excess-profits tax.

This dual relationship of the executive to his job seems, however, to be a passing phase. As business institutions age and expand, they tend to divide the functions of management and ownership. Personal enthusiasm and vigor start business projects, but they proceed toward coöperation under the corporate form, with increasing stress upon order and system. Those which survive several generations usually are found operating under other leadership than that of the owners. Accident of birth may produce owners; but it cannot be depended upon to produce those leaders who must be found if the property is to flourish under competition.

Few of our younger captains of industry own dominant holdings in the corporations they manage; some own no stock in their companies. There is no reason why they should; they are there by reason of their personal powers — their industrial statesmanship. They are actually freer to hold the balance true as against the demands of labor, capital, and the market — their workers, their stockholders and bondholders, and their customers — than they would be if strong financial interest pulled them to one side. Homer Ferguson, president of the Newport News Shipbuilding Company, calls himself a "plain hiredman," owning no part of the property he manages; he has elaborated the reasons why that aloofness from ownership strengthens him in his work. He may

earn less money in his present job than he would earn
running a business of his own; on the other hand, he
has more prestige, greater opportunity. Judge Gary
dominates United States Steel, not by stock-ownership or stock-jobbing, but by the power of a wise and
courageous mind. In his case, too, the chief reward
lies in doing a big work and winning the applause of
the public, not in his salary check. You cannot picture either man, or any other industrial leader worthy
of rank alongside them, as quitting his job in the face
of a salary-cut, or as higgling over the price of his
preferment in the first instance.

In the future, industrial leaders will tend more and
more to be picked men, not owners in any important
sense. Their salaries will depend upon the number
of qualified men in the market, and the existing demand for their services. The lure of such positions,
and the determined efforts being made to educate for
business leadership, are sure to increase the number
of qualified candidates. The demand is, of course,
uncertain; but the chances are that it will not maintain itself relatively to supply, now that education,
both public and private, has set itself to increase the
supply. In that case, the present high level of executive salaries cannot be maintained. All indications
point to the executives of the future carrying their
loads of responsibility less because of the money reward and more because of personal pride and public
spirit. Business leadership seems likely to become a
profession, with professional standards and standing,
as well as professional limitations as to pay.

The learned professions, so-called for tradition's sake, are easier to dispose of, because, in each case, the leveling tendency is reinforced by an established professional ethic. Teachers, preachers, writers and artists generally, for centuries have regarded their wages, not as pay, but as their living, their real rewards being service to their ideals and humanity, established social position, and the regard of their fellow men. These non-economic lures attract human nature so strongly that the rewards in these lines sometimes fall below those of unskilled labor. Poets have starved in garrets; ministers are notoriously underpaid; and of late years comparison of the pinched professor and the silk-shirted yokel has led to "Feed-the-Prof." campaigns.

Law and medicine, because they work more directly upon life, have been more affected by the industrial swirl; but they, too, are bound to swim out of the commercial current to the high ethical shore. Even now, though physicians may talk about their business, they respond to many humanitarian demands; and there exist some lawyers, if not many, who put the eternal cry for justice ahead of fees. So, the leveling influences of automatic machinery are bound to be reinforced and strengthened by the example of professional men, no less than by the teaching of those among them who see service as the high goal of human endeavor.

Thus far we have considered the leveling of labor, as dictated by the automatic tool, solely from the standpoint of production. That is its direct action.

Automatic machinery works indirectly toward the same end, however, through the market — through consumption. As the total cost of the product is the total cost of the brain-labor and hand-labor involved, an immediate effect of production through automatic machines is to reduce the cost of the units produced. The economic advantage of such machinery is so manifest that there can be no stopping its progress short of the point where productive power so far outranges the world's market ability to consume, that further multiplication of man-power is not worth while. No one can foresee whether that point is centuries removed, or merely decades. Theoretically, the capacity of the human race to consume goods is infinite; but actually it is at all times in competition with the universal human demand for leisure. No matter how cheap goods become, there is a point of accumulation beyond which some men will say, "Let's knock off and have some fun." The ranks of labor developed plenty of such cases in 1919.

Short of that point, however, the market repays intensive cultivation. The cheaper goods become, the more of them can be sold, provided purchasing power does not drop coincidentally with prices. It follows that, with increasing automatization in production, competition among sellers of goods on the one hand and buyers of labor-time on the other must push prices and wages toward a point where maximum production and maximum consumption tend to coincide. Such is the variety of human nature and the insistence of human desire that they may never reach absolute coincidence; but the prospects are that they will approach one another with lessening fluctuations. In this country, mass-buying makes the market for most commodities. A broad division of the proceeds of industry stimulates buying far more than a narrow one; hence influences flowing from the sales-end of industry will tend to strengthen that leveling of labor which is predetermined by competition among buyers of labor-power for use on automatic machines.

It must be borne in mind that, under competition, some degree of wage-variation always will exist, from causes lying within the individual, as, for example, the varying wages of operatives under piece-rates. For, while the automatic tool works within a fixed cycle, it is not the precise counterpart of the ancient treadmill. Within narrow and unimportant limits, its productiveness varies somewhat with variations of personal energy and attentiveness. Likewise, there are sure to be variations in different parts of the country, due largely to uneven supply of labor-power resulting from differing local birth-rates and non-economic hindrances to economic shifts of base. Home and family ties, love of one's native environment, stock-ownership by employees, and personal loyalties in work-relations, probably always will influence human beings considerably, and deter them from following the main chance absolutely. Barometric pressure always tends to uniformity, yet is never uniform. The wind blowing where it listeth has its counterpart in the now fluid movement of labor in search of employment, higher pay, or, perhaps, only escape from monotony. Enough men and women can be depended upon to follow the main chance, to effect a fairly even displacement of labor-power and to enforce by economic law a fairly even wage-scale over the entire country.

Not the least interesting part of this leveling tendency is that it runs directly toward that Socialist dream — equality of income. Yet it proceeds without any assistance from the Socialists, solely as the result of the installation of automatic machinery by capitalists. The tendency itself is strictly economic, and conceivably might work out to its ultimate conclusion without calling forth political action, amending the institution of private property, or changing the present relations between employer and employee. Nothing so simple is to be expected; not so easily does humanity accept revolutionary changes in its methods of sustaining life. Farmer-labor parties in the United States and Canada, recently formed, may be taken as evidence of belated appreciation of the economic solidarity of town and country labor under the new conditions of industry.

Woman suffrage gained influence in direct proportion as women became engaged in industrial production. The automatic tool will be the force behind most of our legislation for the next fifty years, just as it will be the mainspring of our educational programme, once its significance is understood by educators still fumbling for the key to modern life. To lads who come as beardless boys into their greatest purchasing power, something must be taught other than has been taught, if they are ever to use their leisure and their economic power aright. The army of homeless, wifeless men and foot-loose women is growing; the automatic tool has cut marriage-knots as well as steel bands. Let all who think in terms of public recreation, domestic relations, charity, religion, morals, child-welfare, and social science ponder those reactions of the automatic tool that daily proceed under their eyes.

In other parts of the world classes are wrestling bloodily for the control of machinery. They are of breeds to whom compromise is difficult. It is our boast that we, as inheritors of the Anglo-Saxon tradition, can settle peaceably clashes of interest over which other humans fight. But we shall never be able to settle peaceably and creditably all the problems arising out of the common use of the automatic tool in industrial production, unless we grasp the social and political possibilities of its evolution.

America gave the automatic tool its chance. Its blessings are evident; but, unless controlled by social conscience, it may develop curses equally potent. America's high duty is to guide the continuing evolution of the Iron Man intelligently. For the economic forces which he releases are of such intense reality and abundant vitality, that they will break governments which blindly oppose them just as quickly as they will undermine societies which yield too supinely to machine dictation. Governments now stake their existences upon controlling men; in the dawning age, the acid test of sovereignty may be control of machines. Through such control the leveling tendency, inherent in automatic production and reinforced by popular education, may be directed toward the goal of true democracy; whereas, undirected, it may push the human race into a new slavery, or stampede it into a new anarchy.

III

MIND AND MACHINE

MEN go to machines under the same compulsions which have sent them into field and forest, ocean lane, and battlefield, since ever the world began — their needs and their instincts. To supply ever-expanding wants with least effort has called forth, from one generation to another, enough ingenuity and adaptability to lift certain breeds from lawless individualists, with scant possessions and moving in restricted circles, into responsible units in a complicated social and industrial order, where life is reasonably secure, where wealth is abundant though unevenly spread, and where the production and distribution of marketable goods proceeds largely through interdependent groupings of many individuals. Within these groups the many work at the direction of the few, under discipline approaching military exactitude, for all that it is based upon bargaining between equals under the law. Leaders and led alike perform certain organically selected functions essential to the group, the community, and the state. Through division of function, through subordination of personalities to leadership in organizations applying force to matter with scientific precision, life has been ameliorated as well as vastly complicated. That this amelioration of life, which we call civilization, is still a going concern, full of vitality, is proved by the very stresses and pains which its innovations rouse.

Continuing attempts by the innovating animal, Man, to feed, clothe, and satisfy himself with the least effort, brought forth naturally, and in process, the application of machinery to production, at first haltingly, but latterly with a rush that finds this generation well on its way to as complete automatization as human nature is capable of sustaining. Economically the course is clear enough—plain sailing between this point and some future point, where men, with minimum effort of mind and muscle, shall do the essential work of the world mechanically, in so far as machinery can be adapted to the task. The limiting force resides, not so much in the ability of our most enterprising selectmen to mechanize the planet, as in their seemingly more restricted ability to make the job appear worth while to those who come to grips with machinery in action — the common folk.

Economic Man is an abstraction essential to scientific inquiry, though nowhere found in the flesh, and, where approximated, not pleasant to have as a neighbor. *Homo sapiens* is social man and political man and religious man as well as economic man. He follows the instinct of self-preservation, not only economically, but also biologically. He loves, mates, breeds, fights for and labors for his wife, his home, his children. And presently he dies, in the hope of an extension of life beyond the grave, and is buried with honor by his kind. In his life he has many governors; among them the state is sovereign and the shop parvenu.

This composite mystery enters the shop, and takes

his place beside the machine, to use a small but definite fraction of his powers in assisting it to produce and distribute goods. Call him Number 3141 if you choose; nevertheless, he differs from numbers 3140 and 3142 and all other men, living or dead. No one, from this time forward to eternity, ever will be cast in exactly the same mould as he. Labor is more than labor; each labor unit is also an individual, immeasurably dear to himself, even in despair.

What the shop precisely wants, it cannot hire. It may want, though never wisely, mere hands and feet and backs; they do not exist detached from lusts, faiths, superstitions. It may want eyes, sensitive fingers, or specialized knowledge; they are not to be divorced from nerves and prejudices. Instead, the labor market presents men and women in infinite variety; but in each is incorporated something, be it little or much, which the shop cannot use. The shop picks and chooses, combs and examines, consults records; nevertheless, the chosen ones carry inside the gates that which may result in an appeal from its regimen to the anarchy of force, or to the authority of the state — the appeal to Demos or to Cæsar.

This mental luggage, largely superfluous from the standpoint of immediate industrial need, may be catalogued for analysis; but the catalogue, however extended, remains a convenient lie, since each element merges with all the others and affects all the others. With this attainder established, the mental luggage of the man going to the machine may be listed briefly as instincts, emotions, traditions, beliefs, habits of thought and conduct — those qualities of mind and spirit which, in their interplay, not only establish the individuality of their possessor, but also govern his reactions to authority and to the responsibilities involved in home and social relationships.

These primary qualities of the mind have their roots in the dawn of life on this planet; in Creation, if you deny Darwin; in intertidal scum, if you accept Wells. But, whatever their origin, they are the fruits of race-experience through many generations; and under the lash of sex we shall pass them on, perhaps with minor changes, to our successors. Our contribution to the subconscious mind is not likely to be as rich and important as the press-agents of our braggart era declare. Indeed, we may influence the subconscious more than any preceding generation, and yet add but a mite to its store, so ancient is its origin and so vital its accumulations. The subconscious mind may be reckoned the reservoir of human experience; here is the cause of Man's rise to command on the planet; here the rough foundations of his social and political institutions; here the explanation, perhaps never to be unraveled, of his greeds, wars, sins, as well as of his virtues, loyalties, and visions.

Subtract the subconscious from high intelligence — the residue is not Man, with his hates and loves, urges and repressions, but a monstrosity of greed and reason. Subtract it from a person of low intelligence; and the result is a semblance of the bestial. Both are asocial; the one, a menace through his efficiency; the other, a menace through his deficiency. Therefore it is of the subconscious mind that one may say, "This is the reality of human existence. The truth about human affairs is not to be found altogether in what is written in the bond and certified to in the records. You must consult the instincts; you must go back to the wells of life. Peer into those misty, uncertain depths diligently enough, and you may get some hint, however faint, of the reality of the human spirit in travail or in joy."

Comes now this heavy-laden, complex Ego to the machine. Pleasant, indeed, for both parties, if the management could separate the workman from such mental luggage as is superfluous inside, and check it at the door, to be reassumed upon return. How simple if the mental man could shuck his cravings as the physical man doffs his coat! Yet, until we know more of the meaning of life, it is perhaps just as well that Man is indivisible, and that the shop must take the useless with the useful, the bitter with the sweet. For it is the unknown and unassayable which gives life its zest, labor its hope, and industry its adventure.

No doubt, those mental traits and prepossessions which we group and label under the convenient title, "subconscious," at one time had clearer economic significance than they possess at present. However men compete for their livings, those attributes which make for survival tend to be passed on, while those less utilitarian are eliminated under the stern pressure of necessity. Every piece of subconscious luggage which the modern carries to the machine must at some time have been of conscious value to enough of his ancestors to fix that trait for survival. Else it must have been sunk without trace in the laborious business of keeping alive.

Labor is the price of life. The tree labors in growth; the field-mouse labors in each search for grain. Man differs from other animals in that he is conscious of his labors and articulate concerning them. Labor-pain stirs him to thought and expression; but he may be even more distressed by, though less conscious of, his indirect labor-strains. Industrial labor-pain, being easily recognized for what it is, can be alleviated or compensated for inside the shop; labor-strain, on the other hand, less simple of diagnosis, has a way of eluding direct action and spreading out and down, until, massed and complicated, it presents itself, not to the principals in their principal relation, but to society and the state — to the principals, that is, in their more remote relations as neighbors and citizens. Labor-pain, by and large, gives us labor problems into which the state injects itself only as a last resort; while broad and continued labor-strain begets social and political problems, powerful cross-currents of opinion, which first agitate the homes of the humble, and in due course agitate the parliaments of the world.

With this distinction between labor-pain and labor-strain established, but remembering always that the twain are more easily separated on paper than in the flesh, let us examine the effect of automatic and semi-automatic machinery upon the minds of its attendants — the mill operatives.

Such machines make relatively small demands upon the wits of their companions; the operative's job is more passive, mentally, than active. Once his limited function is learned, once the man knows how to place standardized material in proper, predetermined fashion, he can earn his pay without further mental effort. He must be attentive, must "dot and carry one" exactly so, because the machine is valuable, and failure to move when and as directed may cost his employer more in spoilage than the operative's yearly wage. The man is not so much driven, as paced; his usefulness depends upon his never failing the strident call of the Iron Man. He nurses his charge, feeds it, relieves it of produce, and perhaps makes slight repairs in a jam. But, if the case is serious, he calls a machinist, just as an infant's nurse calls for the physician in emergency.

I watched a man shove metal rings across six inches of space, to a guide from which they were taken automatically through the machine, emerging slotted some seconds later, without more human ado. That was his job from morning until night, his pay depending upon how many slotted rings passed inspection. Eyes concentrated on his little platform, one hand moving thus, the other so, in unending repetition, he missed not one revolution of the wheels, which were grinding out his life, even as they ground out the goods. Economically he was part of the machine — an automatic feeder, who chanced to be flesh-and-blood-and-mind. Presently, no doubt, he will be relieved of that particular job by a mechanical extension of that particular Iron Man, since the human was doing nothing that could not be done better by metal in motion.

Assembling of interchangeable machined parts proceeds, in efficient plants, with almost equally minute division of function. Your automobile frame, let us say, is hoisted so that it may acquire axles. Then it moves along a conveyer, before gangs of men, each of whom performs thereon a certain specified task for which just so much time is allowed, because the conveyer moves at a fixed rate of speed, and each gang is allotted a space alongside, and moves forward and back in that space as the conveyer works. One attaches the right front-wheel; another the left rear-wheel; a third tightens certain screws with a pneumatic wrench. Let a single human fail in his assignment, and rather than permit that delay to clog the whole line of cars in process, the lagging unit is pulled out of line, to await the next shift. Thus, within an hour from the time a naked frame starts down the assembly line, a shrewd and swiftly moving division of labor has completed thereon a finished motor-car, capable of moving to the loading docks under its own power. Its power-plant has been both painted and dried within the hour. To it have been given a body highly polished, curtains, cushions, tools, and, finally, a tag setting it apart for someone near or far — Doc Kennicott of Gopher Prairie, or the Gaekwar of Baroda.

In that swift progress hundreds of men have worked upon each car, combining into effectiveness the work of other thousands, whose produce is brought up by truck from storerooms and source-factories, and rushed into assigned positions. Each man performs the same task over and over: tightens identical nuts, lifts identical parts off a rack, and applies each one of them precisely to a something that is exactly like its predecessor to the thousandth of an inch. This accurate, monotonous toil goes on swiftly, amid hissing air-valves and paint-streams, roar of drying ovens, clatter of tools, thunder of trucks arriving and departing. As evidence of the organizing faculty in master minds, as a study in unity and synchronized power over divers beings and things, the action is impressive, in totality almost beautiful; but for its individual contribution it leaves something to be desired as an expression of the art of life. Not altogether for this, surely, is man made.

Some of these operations involve much muscular effort, others little; but, whether little or much, each operative uses the same set of muscles, for approximately the same length of time, in each repetition of his assigned operation. Roustabouts enjoy far more of the luxury of variety in toil than machine tenders in automatized factories.

The operating of automatic and semi-automatic machinery evolves evidence tending to show that fatigue, instead of being simply weariness from muscles stretched too much or too often, is rather a pathological condition, due to the poisoning of the system through oversecretion of the endocrinal glands. Whatever the theorizing as to endocrinal glands,

it is probably true that there is an excessive out-
pouring under nervous tension, when effort is prolonged beyond the normal fatigue limit, which out-
pouring causes pathological fatigue, indicated by
preternatural activity. This theory, held by competent investigators, and advanced by them with reservations proper in a matter where exactness is difficult,
seems to explain, as well as receive support from, many
of the reactions of our industrial operatives to their
labors.

In general, machine-production of goods involves
less muscular and sensory strain than that put forward under the handicraft system. Fatigue in industrial workers must be ascribed more to monotony
in movement and problem than to foot-pounds of
energy expended. One may use merely his finger-tips
feeding metal discs into a machine, and yet be as
weary in the evening as if he had been swinging an
axe. The lumberjack's weariness is an all-round
fatigue, and he is ready for bed at sundown; whereas
industrial workers seem moved to abnormal activity
after working hours. My fellow citizens, most of
whom work in factories where the industrial function
is minutely divided, and where machines set the pace,
display astonishing energy in after-work pursuits.
The married men reëstablish their equilibrium by
gardening prodigiously, and tinkering furiously
around their homes — a socially satisfactory adjustment. The homeless rush hither and thither by motor
when they are flush; or wander aimlessly around the
streets when they are broke. Books and quiet con-

versation are a bit too tame for men who feel that, while they get their livings in the shop, they must live their lives outside the shop.

This may be explained as Nature's effort to correct a nerve-distortion resulting from the exercise of certain muscles and faculties while all others are held out of use. Glandular secretions, roused by an over-stressed fraction of the anatomy, spread beyond that fraction, to stimulate the rest of the man into heightened activity. These men are in a condition parallel to that in which many a business man finds himself after prolonged concentration upon a problem which defies satisfactory solution. He becomes too tired to sleep; works feverishly; and, unless he lets down, breaks down. Either type is apt to seek relief in stimulants, and to crave thrills temporarily blotting out the discontent that overlays their lives.

At the root of this discontent lies the difficulty of adjusting human beings to modern industry. Race-inheritance fits us for other, simpler pursuits. For unnumbered generations we white folks have been building up resistance to, and recovering from, the fatigue which follows muscle-labor. Except for the comparatively small fraction of our ancestors who went in for learning, trade, or the handicrafts, the life of the masses, until the Industrial Revolution began in England, about 1765, had been the slow life of soil and water — agriculture, hunting and fishing, with occasional relapses into war; occupations requiring intense physical exertion through short periods, and allowing frequent let-ups. Until so recently Man worked by the sun and the seasons, instead of by the calendar and the clock. Even the villein ploughing his lord's glebe could stop for a chat with his neighbor passing on the highway. Thrills a-plenty filled common lives; there were the touch-and-go of the chase; rustic ceremonies at seed-time and harvest; a chance to look in through the servant's door upon the festivities of the manor-house; and always a close, if servile, relation with his boss. Bond the villein was, but his bond held both ways — upon master no less than upon man. The worker at least had the blessing of security in his job, now so uncertain; he could not be fired, even as he could not hire himself away.

That simple existence seems to be the kind of life for which the common man is constituted. Physically, he goes his best gait for a hundred yards, fells his third tree more accurately than he fells his thirtieth, ploughs his straightest furrow toward the rising sun. He needs a measure of monotony in toil; shifting at quick-step from this job to that bothers him; but the work which gives him most satisfaction, and which, all things considered, he does best, is that furnishing variety in detail with sameness in essentials. Were every tree placed exactly like every other tree, to be felled from a like stance in the one direction, with no nice problem of adjustment presenting itself to the common sense and skill of the axe-man, then our lumberjack would return to his shack, not only more fatigued in body than usual, but infinitely more weary in his mind. If a high-grade carpenter faced

the prospect of building identical houses all the rest
of his life, with never a chance to revel in a bit of im-
provisation, would he relish that prospect? Hardly.
What he wants — what every man above the grade
of moron craves in toil — is a chance to express his
personality within the limits of a specialty in which
he knows himself proficient. Even the scavenger is
not without his craft-pride. Your carpenter desires
no other trade; he would rather build a hen-coop
than paint his own dwelling; but inside his trade he
wants a bit of leeway to devise ways and means, and
a living hope of quiet adventure. Not enough variety
to upset him, but enough to stimulate the exercise of
his full powers in security — such is the common
man's ideal job.

Variety in minors compensates for the major
monotony. In the beginning, and for æons thereafter,
when Man, in an environment niggardly in food and
crowded with dangers, was "getting set" in build and
character, labor — the price of life — must have been
a constant succession of adventures. Merely keeping
alive involved prowling and stalking, sally, pounce,
battle, flight. Power to put all into a single effort
determined whether one returned to the home-lair or
died miserably on the heath.

Little by little, to satisfy accumulating economic
wants and social ambitions, Man tied himself down
to occupations more prosaic — to agriculture, to the
tedious shaping of tools from stone, and the application of manual skill and fire to earth-materials.
Ability to withstand monotony then acquired sur-

vival value; but there continued that zest for variety inside the frame of monotony, that desire to project his unique self upon his environment.

From the projection of these individualities upon matter through toil followed many of the subsequent changes in Man's estate. Simple tools, now standardized, must have measured the individuality of their originators and adapters, just as innovations in modern mechanics publish to a critical world the personal triumphs of those who dare to originate. The more play we allow this instinct for variation, the swifter economic evolution must be; and, conversely, when it has no play, innovation ceases. Civilization, on its material side, has been built little by little, through trial and error rather than design — by the personal energies of the world's artificers and organizers rather than by the plans of its statesmen.

Monotony in labor, then, is the price men pay for living together in order and security — one of the returns that society exacts from the individual in exchange for safety, comfort, and opportunity for advancement within the group. But monotony intensifies labor-strain; and unless the laborer can find release therefrom, through variations of physical and mental effort in the minutiæ of the job, his weariness sits upon him like an incubus.

Let him do this thing a little differently from that; let him use what ingenuity he has; and his Ego, somewhat different from all others under the sun, is compensated in a degree for the surrender of his freedom in the larger concerns of group-living, which surrender society demands and enforces through law and custom.

But, lacking this compensation of variety in toil, human nature finds the social order oppressive. This seems to me at least as definite a cause of the present resentment against the established order as those more frequently cited; and the situation is not altogether relieved by reflecting that, as long as the instinct toward variation is repressed by the machines themselves, its consequences will continue in some measure as long as machines are operated, no matter whether they are owned by private persons or by the state.

How long may a person's innovating tendencies be repressed without dulling his mind? Suppose our first-rate carpenter undertook a two-year stint laying identical floors in identical one-story houses. Would he be as good an all-round craftsman, as good a stair-builder and roof-builder, at the end of his grind? Obviously not. He might grow more deft in what he had to do; but surely he would grow more clumsy in what he had no chance to do. He would emerge from that job less efficient for the all-round work of the community, less sure of himself, less secure in his home and his living, less interesting as a personality and less valuable as a neighbor and citizen. To what extent this decline in the individual might affect his descendants, and through them the race, is an interesting question reserved for future discussion. Here the influence of automatic machinery upon the mind of those who come into close and continued contact with it is considered only with relation to the present actors immediately involved, without reference to the extension of that influence through heredity and race-evolution.

This devolution of the individual is what Secretary Hoover notes when he says: "The vast, repetitive processes are dulling the human mind." And again: "We must take account of the tendencies of our present repetitive industries to eliminate the creative instinct in their workers, to narrow their fields of craftsmanship, to discard entirely the contributions that could be had from their minds as well as from their hands. Indeed, if we are to secure the development of our people, we cannot permit the dulling of these sensibilities."

So far as the great majority of the workers are concerned, modern industry presents this phenomenon — the dulling of the mind — on a scale unequaled in extent, and to a degree unequaled in intensity, by anything on record in history. Slavery of the galley was not more uninspiring, *per se*. Military orders may be more imperious than those of industry; but at least the military life provides change of scene and problem from time to time, some release from routine on pay, much companionship, and occasional thrills — all appealing to the common man because they fit in so neatly with the inherited memories lying at the back of his mind. Industrial efficiency calls for the elimination of many of these boons — for close concentration upon the unvarying task, for suppression of variations in toil, for rigid control of the work-environment, for elimination of distracting excitements, for subordination of personalities, for the reduction of the common man to the status of automaton.

Who is this common man? He is the fellow who made up the ranks of the army as examined for the draft — an adult male — with an intelligence, by test, of from fourteen to sixteen years. He is a dependable being on the average, capable of taking care of himself and his family in ordinary times and not too complicated situations; fairly adaptable; amenable to law and social usages; requiring and accepting leadership in all pursuits calling for special knowledge or quick decision; fundamentally loyal to his country and its institutions; inherently conservative and provincial; shaking down after the first flush of youth into a steady, plodding citizen, more prone to excitement over little things than to thought over fundamentals; strongly sexed, but controlling his sex-calls more or less successfully with the aid of church and state, of which institutions he is ever the pillar and support. Not a complete portrait, but 't will serve!

This is he who, in the main, mans industry; and upon whom modern industry grinds. It grinds less upon those definitely above or below this level. More effective, more adaptable persons, keen in devising, sage in planning, and strong in pushing men and materials into action — these find in industry broad and lucrative outlets for their relatively stronger instincts toward dominance. Industry gives them opportunity to express their egos in great works, to lead, to build, to amass, to commandeer social recognition through the exercise of economic power. Men of this sort find capital, invent machines, improve processes, route materials, organize shops, produce goods in quantity, and sell them to the ends of the earth. Their methods are direct, often ruthless; their code an odd mixture of jungle law and altruism. No danger of repetitive processes and automatic machinery dulling these high-powered minds; on the contrary, these are as manna to their hungry souls. By reducing room for error in operations, by contracting the play of human fallibility in toil, by increasing man-power, the Iron Man has freed business of important limitations, relieving enterprisers of what were once serious difficulties.

But the slack so gained is more apparent than real. Competition, never resting, drives them on ever and ever to more refined machines, better coördination of effort; and presently they find in social unrest, plant obsolescence, high labor-turnover, and lowered morale, that they have merely substituted one sort of executive vexation for another. In the old days of more skill and less machines, the executive problem was to master materials; now the executive problem is to a much greater degree the handling of men.

Neither does the Iron Man get on the nerves of those below the average mentality. He is a consistent friend of the defective. Just as deafness is an advantage in certain industrial occupations, — our shops employ many mutes with satisfaction both ways, — so mental lacks may become assets for certain industrial purposes. Given enough sense to master simple routine occupations, and enough appreciation of duty, or fear of relatives, to come to the shop regularly, the below-average person can soon be adjusted industrially. And, when adjusted, the moron will be found immune to many of the pricks which irritate the normal man into seeing red, less fretted by monotony, less worn by rhythmic clatter. There is less in his soul striving to release itself; he has brought into the shop comparatively little that the shop cannot use; and so he accepts dumbly his appointed place in the scheme of things industrial, remains unbitten by ambition, and reacts not at all against subordination. The less mind one has, the less it resents that invasion of personality which is inseparable from large-scale and mechanized enterprises. I have heard industrial engineers and welfare workers say that industrial efficiency, as working out in our day, puts a premium on mental deficiency.

Men who take more to the machines than do the morons are subjected to a rigid selective process by the Iron Man. The law of "use or lose" begins its inexorable operation upon their minds as well as upon their muscles and nerves. Just as muscle or nerve, unused, refuses to yield its utility without a struggle, causing its possessor pain and inconvenience, so those mental qualities unused in toil continue to struggle for existence to the limit of their strength. It is easy to find in any industrial town the shop-sick man — upset, out of sorts, doubtful if he can stick it out. The man is out of harmony with himself; his mind is divided against itself. The weaker the Ego at the start, the shorter the struggle, and the more quickly does the individual become "shop-broke." Some refuse to wait so long, and get out, either fired for insubordination, which is more often an attack of "nerves" than meanness, or going out voluntarily to search for jobs more to their liking. Sometimes they merely shift from one shop to another; every factory town has its disappointed rainbow-chasers, who never stay put, and who never learn that the Iron Man is about the same everywhere. Many, however, drift back to the farm and other less mechanized occupations.

Labor-turnover is heavy; that is where this labor-strain shows in the shop records. The workman and his boss may adjust, in one way or another, disputes on wages and shop-conditions; but of necessity they have difficulty in treating this intangible, indefinite, not always recognized, or recognizable, work-neurosis arising from the cleavage between old and new, between the innovation — the Iron Man — and that ancient inheritance of the human — the mind. So one man goes, and another, and another; their several departures, listed together, become evidence of so many loss-items to the shop. The expense of breaking in a single novice may be small; but multiplied many times, it becomes something to reckon with in quantity, and a definite economic back-lash. Moreover, the departure of even a single cog in the synchronized process of production, where many await the output of one machine, may delay production, at a cost far in excess of the direct expense of substituting the human factor. Let a key-machine be idle even a few hours, and bang goes far more than sixpence!

So the leaders of industry are forced, from strictly economic motives, to consider the psychological aspects of toil. The remedies they apply are of infinite variety,— shifting men from one job to another as an antidote for monotony and a cure for maladjustments; more rigid selection in employment, with growing emphasis on the mental as well as physical fitness of the novices for the jobs open; welfare-work in all its phases; housing developments, grievance committees, shop-councils, employee representation, bonus and profit-sharing plans,— all aimed at relieving in one way or another, either directly or by distraction of interest, the nerve-tension under which the average man suffers when he is brought into double harness with the Iron Man.

However, the best friend of both man and master, in this connection, is habit — simple, old-fashioned habit. If one does the same thing over and over, action tends to become automatic. Attention may be trained through use, even to the point where the tender of the machine may do his work accurately without undue strain, while his mind busies itself elsewhere. The strain increases, of course, as the work is prolonged; but given reasonable time-limits, there is ground to believe that a man, thoroughly shopbroken and well adjusted to his job, may get a good deal of pleasure from this autistic thinking while at work. But autistic thinking may be painful as well as pleasurable. The day-dreaming of a well-balanced, not too highly organized mind, at peace with itself and with the world, is one thing; the fretting of a mind under worry or injustice is quite another.

If we conceive habit to be a barrier behind which the mind may shelter itself against fatigue, then we may say that the assaulting force must succeed, if the work-period be stretched unduly; and, moreover, that it will carry the habit-barrier much sooner than that, if the mental forces behind the barrier are discordant and undisciplined. Consequently, the constructive effort to harmonize automatic machinery and mental health must take a threefold path: first, to select individuals carefully for given jobs; second, to adjust both pace and hours to the individual's powers of resisting fatigue; and, third, to hasten such changes in the shop, home, and community as will tend to content the common man with his lot, reduce his worry and envy, and increase his delight in life.

At the automatic machine a man must stew, mentally, in his own juice; in so far as he thinks at all, his thought must range away from his task. If he fears dismissal, if he thinks of himself as bested by unknown forces or cheated by individuals, if he finds himself and his home the playthings of tragedy or the butts of injustice, then his autistic thought is bound to be subversive. One sort of man becomes melancholy; another rages against things as they are. On the other hand, he whose life is even and sustained by faith, he whose memories and prospects are alike pleasurable, has time inside the task to plan his holiday,

turn over again the delights of last week, and settle the
small but inspiring problems of his home and garden.

To put the machine operative into this frame of
mind, where he is insulated more or less against the
early coming and more devastating inroads of pathological fatigue, must ever be a first concern of industrial society, as well as of the shop which profits
by his content. The state must do its bit by seeing
that he gets full measure of justice; the community,
by providing facilities for mental and physical recreation; and the shop, by internal adjustments calculated
to increase the worker's confidence in the security of
his job and his sense of coöperation in the enterprise.

All important, also, is the cultivation of self-dis-
cipline in the individual. Much restlessness arises
from envy, lack of disposition to make the best of
things until better appears, and failure to train the
emotions toward cheerfulness. Mental hygiene in
home and school is a positive need for a rising generation destined so largely to associate with machines
and coöperate in large-scale enterprises.

How the emotions may be schooled is set forth
briefly in Dr. C. B. Burr's trenchant little book,
" Practical Psychology and Psychiatry," now in its
fifth edition — a mine of wisdom! " The relation of
emotion in the abstract to muscular expression is
profitable for study," says Dr. Burr, " not only because of its psychological interest, but because of its
practical bearing upon human conduct. Clench the
fist and shut the teeth firmly, and there immediately
arises in consciousness a sense of resentment, of pug-

nacity. Draw down the corners of the mouth, and the emotional tone takes on a shade of depression. This has an important relation to mental development. To cultivate the muscular play that accompanies pleasurable states of feeling must inevitably affect the disposition of the individual in a favorable manner." Thus, he who does the necessary with a show of willingness finds, before the task is done, that he is truly willing its accomplishment.

"Be good and you'll be happy" is a precept of practical religion. "Make good or you'll be miserable" is a precept of business which seems to have crowded the older ideal out of public education, and to have jostled it sadly, even in the home. An educational system overemphasizing efficiency must needs wreck itself in time, because there can never be quite enough of the good things of life at hand to satisfy all. A homely philosophy of give-and-take, a gospel of endurance as contrasted with acquisition, the truth that life's best values are spiritual rather than economic — these the school should teach, no less than the home, to young folk who presently shall take their places beside the machines in industrial routine.

Yet such preparation will not be sufficient of itself. As those once more potent ideals of contentment in toil have been pushed aside so strenuously by industrialism, so also they cannot be rehabilitated in any compelling measure until the industrial *status quo* is modified by state, community, and shop, in such wise that training for contentment may withstand the attrition of work-relations in adult years. As long as life reneges on promises made to youth that joy, honor, and abundance shall reward toil, sobriety, and loyalty, it is idle to expect any generation of American factory-hands to bear stoically their participation in industry.

However successful these efforts may be, there is likely to remain an unavoidable residuum of labor-strain. This, spread as it is over the mass, filters down upon home and state, generating social problems which, in a democracy, shortly become political. In our average man, as we have seen, the will to survive is more potent than the will to power; security means more to him than opportunity; he is static rather than dynamic; and the state is the highest expression of his dominant ideal — to live comfortably under conditions in which he can be true to his not-too-demanding nature. To the state, therefore, the man of the masses gives, as clearly as he can, his mandate. First, labor-strain rouses thought, then speech, then writings in the press, then debates in parliament, then — if checkmated all along the line — in mobs and armies. The politician with his ear to the ground serves this function, at least — he gets the case of the plebs before the state. Ensues then a new phase of the old, old duel between the state and the captains — going forward in our day as the state *versus* its legal children, the Corporations, in which the captains, for greater power and profit, group themselves.

One finds in the current phase of this contest small promise that the state, by legal processes, can relieve

the common man from the labor-strains incident to
automatic production. It may relieve his feelings
temporarily, with restrictions that are more noise than
substance; he may draw some comfort from seeing
the state crack its long whip over the boss; but political coercion has its limits, both economic and
constitutional. Regulation toward fair play in industry is right and proper, but may so easily be over-
done that the state's most telling contribution to the
mental hygiene of industry may be considered that
of education — the marshaling of the public schools
for the teaching of contentment in toil and culture in
leisure.

Because mind must be cured by mind, or stay sick,
because human maladjustments yield only to the
human touch, the mental phase of the problem of
automatization in industry challenges particularly
the community and the shop; to them we must look
for the chief ameliorating influences which shall permit the common man to withstand, without deteriora-
tion of mind, association with the Iron Man. And
because the man at the desk moves more swiftly than
the folk in the town-meeting, the shop may well
become the more effective of the two. Once management grasps clearly the situation created by the
grinding of the automatic machine upon the mind of
the worker, the challenge to proximate service and
ultimate interest can not but inspire the directing
intelligences of American industry. Their hegemony,
indeed, depends upon their leaping into this breach
without delay.

IV
THE IRON DUKES

THE more monotonous the plain, the more impressive are the peaks. As the development and growing use of machinery reduce, little by little, the play of personality in toil for the masses who work beside it, those who rise above its leveling influences take on increased social significance. As labor becomes more and more impersonal, as labor-time crowds out skill and initiative as the chief economic determinant of the mass, those who can take advantage of this situation to employ or direct large numbers of individuals stand out as marked men. They are the stars of the industrial drama. Upon them the limelight beats; upon them are showered applause and riches in such profusion as to rouse the envy of the chorus. For them, too, are the hisses sometimes heard in the pit, and occasional missiles launched in wrath.

Ability heads toward power. When the big business of the country was the establishing, organizing, and defending of the state, supremely able men turned their talents toward statecraft, just as, in former times and older lands, they went into the church when religion was esteemed the path toward greatest influence. When the political stability of this Republic had been achieved, America's ablest organizers were attracted, naturally, to the prospect of power attainable through exploiting the natural resources of an undeveloped continent. Their imaginations fired, they went overseas for capital, built railroads, razed forests, made goods, and improved methods of marketing.

Desire to win subsistence and make the futures of themselves and their families secure may have been the tap-root of these undertakings; but there were sturdy brace-roots as well — the urge to build, to create, to coördinate; the will to power, to prominence, to dominance. Even the roughest of these economic adventurers could scarcely escape being stirred somewhat by the thought that what he was doing was of service to his fellows, and would continue to be of service long after he himself had vanished from the stormy scene. He and his kind must have been sustained, at many points in their none too easy lives, by that faith seldom put into words. Less glib, surely, than our generation in talking "service," such men served posterity as well as themselves and their legatees.

We see now that men like Stephenson and Hill, Maudslay and McCormick, Bessemer and Carnegie, made something more than money by harnessing natural forces, perfecting machines, and organizing men and capital into effective combinations for laying rails, running trains, fabricating steel, and selling reapers. They pioneered for civilization. While some of them gathered vast fortunes for themselves and their heirs, each did his bit toward lifting the economic level for whole groups and sections, enriched and extended his country, and gave life in such abundance that the population of the earth doubled within a single century of industrial control. We know that these men, and thousands of other leaders in the economic development of the Western world, possessed high survival value. Their works live; their contributions are still being used; they released certain energies of nature and man, never again to be prisoned; and all of us are distinctly their heirs and debtors. Indeed, a good half of us could not find a living, a foothold on earth, but for them and their kind.

Individual achievements broaden down in time to social assets. The mass inherits what the class creates, whereupon the class carries on to a new objective. The process is seen clearly enough in the case of the railroads. The state is now the overlord, and masses of small holders are the owners, of railroads which dominant individuals built, because the state would not accept responsibility for construction. The state chose—and the common sense of the time approved— to let private persons adventure in providing steam transportation. The common sense of our time approves payment of rental to those who have come into possession of those holdings; but it still refuses to take the risk of operation, while determined to hold the rewards of operation down to fixed limits by rate-control.

In the railroad-building era, enterprising youth and far-visioned men went to the rails as deer to the salt-licks — because it was their nature so to do. No calm process of reasoning directed their choice of life-work. They plunged into that "game" instinctively, because it seemed the most worth-while of all pursuits, the field in which a man could most nearly realize all that was in him. Men of the same sort plunged, in a later generation, into electric transportation — first urban, then interurban. In the last twenty years many of them have gone into industry, into what we call interchangeable manufacturing, but which the Germans, with their penchant for verbal exactness, call *"Mechanofabrik"* — the quantity production of standardized goods on power-driven machines, and the distribution thereof over wide areas. And latterly, when it became apparent that the financing of quantity production and wide distribution was a function so important to society that it returned both profits and power, such went into banking also. Indeed, industry could scarcely have reached its present proportions if banks and bankers had not grown with it.

The reasons for the shifting of our self-appointed captains — our ablest practical-minded citizens — from statecraft, through transportation, to industry are not far to seek. The state not only had been securely founded, but also had grown strong enough to inject itself firmly — through federal, state and local governments—into the business equation as a regulatory force.

The will to power always mates ill with state control. The transportation field had been pioneered, opportunity for profitable adventuring in that line reduced; but thereby ways and means had been created to distribute goods widely and swiftly. Population had increased, and the standard of living risen. In other words, a broad and absorbent market existed, into which cheap goods could be poured at a profit.

The incentive, consequently, was present, to apply as swiftly as might be the idea of skill-transference to machines, "so that unskilled workmen," to quote Roe, "might be made to produce the same results as skilled labor." This shift of vital function from the worker to the tool inevitably engaged the attention of men keen to exercise the realities of power, since it enabled larger numbers and more capital to be concentrated, organized, and commanded by a single directing mind.

Though automatic machinery had to await the market for its goods before becoming common enough to gain marked social significance, which occurred coincidentally with the slowing-up of railroad-building in the eighteen-eighties, the idea of skill-transference appears far earlier, and was applied here and there. Sir Samuel Bentham, brother of Jeremy, faced with the problem of building and outfitting ships on the Black Sea, for Catherine the Great of Russia, in a territory containing few skilled artisans, practised "skill-transference," with some success, as early as 1787. Back in England, with the help of Brunel and Maudslay, he later applied it on a large scale, in a new factory for the interchangeable manufacture of ship-blocks at Portsmouth (1808).

Meanwhile, Eli Whitney, at New Haven, was equally alert. Seeking a small-arms contract in 1812, Whitney wrote to Washington of his plant, that "its great leading object is to substitute correct and effective operations of machinery for that skill of the artist which is acquired only by long practice and experience, a species of skill which is not possessed in this country to any appreciable extent." Those who would delve further into the hazy beginnings of the Machine Age are referred to J. W. Roe's "English and American Tool-Builders," an excellent piece of research in a supremely important field.

That olden, far-off note of enthusiasm for the machine-escape from human ineptness was sounded again, after more than a century, by Karl W. Zimmerscheid, Vice-President of the General Motors Company, in these words:—

"The most potent single factor in the brilliant rise of the mechanical industry in America is the almost universal adoption of the principles of interchangeable manufacture. There are underlying economic reasons for the opportunities which have arisen continually before us; but no nation with so few skilled mechanics as ours ever would have taken advantage of those opportunities so adequately, without possessing the genius to conceive the idea of assembling things from parts wholly produced by automatic machinery; nor could even such genius have brought success, had the final conception failed to include the masterly yet simple provision that all such automatically produced parts should be so alike as to be perfectly interchangeable from one assembly to another. Given this system in its present stage of development, problems of vast quantity production at remarkably low costs, of easy and rapid assembly, and of inexpensive maintenance, become fascinating play. The seeming miracles of such intricate, though widespread, products as the sewing machine, the harvester, the dollar watch, the talking machine, and the automobile, become but the obvious fruits of a natural evolution."

This may be fascinating play for the directing minds, but it is the reverse of fascinating for those who operate the machines; and hard, solid work, not play, for the social workers and statesmen who somehow must ameliorate the effects of the Iron Man, lest the race degenerate, society collapse, and the twin pillars of the modern state — constitutionalism and private property — be torn asunder. Scarcely, either, are those financiers enthusiastic who must wrestle with the credit problems arising from over-production or under-consumption — whichever you choose to saddle with responsibility for the post-war glut of goods turned out under direction of our fascinated, almost hypnotized, players in the game of business.

It is the pleasant habit of biographers, presenting successful men to the public gaze, to emphasize the superior ratiocination of their subjects. *A* succeeded in this great project because he made a wise decision at a certain stage in his career; *B*, because of his persistence in fighting for what seemed to be a lost cause, which he alone of all men knew must be ultimately victorious. Of course, we cannot eliminate intellect altogether as a source of strength in competition; but with superiors, as with the common run of folks, reason usually comes in to justify and explain decisions already made on the basis of the emotions. James J. Hill, for instance, went into railroading because he was a dreamer of dreams; his nature reacted instinctively to the challenge of the broad Dakota prairies. Colt clung to his idea of a pistol with a revolving cartridge-chamber, when other men gave theirs up, because he was more obstinate than they, not because he had better reasoning faculties. The hero of W. L. George's "Caliban," a capital study of the driving type in modern industry, is exceedingly human in this, that he is more emotional than rational.

The superior mind, of the sort attracted by the mill and the market-place, soon establishes its superiority in an environment where the satisfaction of material wants is of prime importance to society. This dominant type of mind may be more difficult to analyze than the mediocre mind, but the difference is one of degree rather than of kind, since all men — and women, too — dominate as far as they can. Intellect and training are worth while in boss-ship; but when one of our chief industrial leaders boasts of his ignorance of history, art, and philosophy, and manages his commercial undertakings well, *minus* those backgrounds, we must agree that other factors weigh somewhat heavier.

No analysis of this type of mind can be complete; but its high spots are plain. First, the universal instinct to dominate is highly developed. The man is the child of the lad who ran around the corner in advance of his mates — first in their play, first in their mischief, also. As he develops, he shows a determination to amount to something out of the ordinary; some invisible goad spurs him on to efforts which to the unambitious average man seem little short of

superhuman. Then the fellow shows marked adaptability. Your picked man, who picks himself, has a
superior elasticity. Down to-day, he is up to-morrow;
backed into a corner, he dodges out; thwarted in one
direction, he tries, undismayed, another tack. His
eye ever on the goal, he twists round many a sharp
corner while the wiseacres are predicting disaster. He
comes quickly to decisions, and takes prompt advantage of chance developments. Circumstance, a run of
luck, underlying economic causes, over which he has
no control and which he perhaps does not even understand—these may determine the extent of his fortune
and influence; yet the man himself must be credited
with daring to put himself in their path, come weal,
come woe.

Experience is his chief school; but it is one in which
he soaks in lessons like a sponge. But, equally important are his gift of getting and holding confidence,
and his ability to pick men for their jobs and keep
them working together, in spite of personal and professional jealousies. He must be at once a captain, a
coach, and a field-marshal, dealing with all sorts and
conditions of men, binding them together in loyalty to
himself and the business group. He is a general who
maintains discipline in his army, not through power of
life or death and the prestige of the state, but by using
justly his power of the purse and exerting fairly the
pressure of his personality. Indeed, power of purse
avails him only with the weak; and it is the strong he
must have with him to save his institution unimpaired
in the daily battle of the market-place.

So, from whatever standpoint you analyze the mental traits of industrial leaders, you come round to the common-sense, blanket explanation of their success — personality; always a riddle to read, and here so often electrified by a mystic current of uncertain voltage; now almost dormant, now searingly alive. They do because they are, and favoring circumstances so reinforce their efforts that there is no stopping them. Sometimes they overdo, whereupon more sober, commonplace men reap where they have sown. No matter, they have made their contribution.

In our days these men exert immense power. One such may hold power of the purse over hundreds of thousands of workers and their dependents. Within limits set by economics on one hand and law on the other, he influences their standard of living, their homes, their diet, the education of their children; whether he pays high wages or low, takes on or lays off help, he influences real-estate values and the general prosperity in many communities, and through them the tax-moneys available for schools, parks, playgrounds, and other such compensations for the social sacrifices inherent in industrial processes.

Again, within the limits set by economic law, what he brings to market and the price he puts upon it affect the well-being of millions of consumers here and abroad. One such man can change the character of a community in five years; transform a quiet country village into an American Essen in ten; uproot thousands of farm-hands from their birth-areas and put them to tending machines; educate whole peoples in wants; and, in short, shift our world somewhat from what it was economically, socially, politically. Our earth, with petroleum-burning China on its breast, is not what it was before Standard Oil cultivated that market. From whatever aspect you look at them, these are the key-men of the present generation. Without them we should not be what we are.

Every industrial community knows its leaders. They are the men behind the pay-rolls. If the big boss, as usually happens, is courting capital in New York, or the state in Washington, or orders in the market-place, or pleasure at Palm Beach, then his chief deputy speaks with the voice of authority. Main Street — the bankers and business and professional men — knows who's who; likewise the politicians and the press. Of course the work-folk know; they feel the reality of things too well to have illusions on that score. The best story a steel-town paper can print is the one that concerns Gary; the Duponts are now prime news in General-Motors towns, where the name scarcely had been heard before the World War. Get the names of the men behind the pay-roll on your petitions, and the rest is easy. Aldermen withdraw their opposition to public improvements, boards of education reverse themselves overnight, at the sight of those puissant signatures. Mayors are not averse to consulting with factory heads on matters pertaining to the general welfare; and the advice they receive, in all matters not affecting the corporate interest directly, is apt to be thoroughly sane and sound.

Useless to pout about this deference shown the industrial leaders of the community. It is rooted deep in reality. The fact is, that any man who exercises such power over the community becomes more than a private citizen. He is a public man, *ipso facto*, and is treated as such. He means as much to his town as the lord in his castle meant to the mediæval community clustered about its rocky base; probably more, since he is less the tax-gatherer and more the coöperator. Through him, in the last analysis, the community functions; through him it gets its goods to market; through him it draws the wherewithal for upkeep, security, growth. The masses may hate their master, or feel toward him admiration akin to love; but whatever their feeling, they have common sense enough to recognize his mastery, and to accept his leadership in the vital concerns of communal life.

The analogy with feudalism can be carried further in the larger industrial cities where are many leaders. Community of interest and taste tends to draw the industrial leaders together into a sort of rough-hewn, dominating oligarchy. Like all oligarchies, it has its inside feuds; sometimes there is even a persistent rebel, like Ford in Detroit; but usually, in those matters in which industry touches the community, industrial leaders will be found presenting a united front. This unity manifests itself, naturally enough, in defending property, combating "agitators" and upholding law and order.

But, where these primary interests are not challenged too seriously, the enterprisers frequently originate and push through to completion social-reform measures of the highest value to the people. After all, they are citizens, with vast appetites for improvement, lusting after progress, and chronically out of patience with the slow, feckless methods of government. They are all for getting things done, and not at all averse to standing well with their fellows. So, from a variety of motives, ranging from lofty ideals of service, through personal vanity, down to sheer self-interest in placating the plebs, they initiate, found, and finance all manner of good works — hospitals, charities, clinics, art galleries, symphony orchestras, even as the grandees of olden Europe.

The people, as older peoples have done, take these things calmly, as a matter of course, without displaying too much interest, unless hurried too fast; whereupon they react by voting down a perfectly good charter, or something of the sort, simply to prove that they do not like to be hustled too briskly along the path of progress.

The leaders of our greatest corporations, in their powers, and their social significance to industrial society, are modern counterparts of the dukes in days when dukes had power. Duke, from *dux*, from *ducere* — to lead. Our dukes have won their power in competition of the stiffest; or, if coming to leadership by easier means, they keep it by their talents for ordering and governing. Their dukedoms are holding-corporations, under whose authority are ranged "held" corporations, captained by lesser chiefs, each aspiring, in the grim old human way, for higher place and power. A half-dozen such recently rebelled against a new boss, and followed their old chief out into a new venture, as boldly as Bonnie Dundee rode out of Edinburgh town.

The dukes have their official cabinets and their expert advisers, not only in the special concerns of business, but in their broader relations with society, which provide them with markets, labor, funds. They have their economists, psychologists, publicity agents, chaplains. Injecting ministers into departments of personal relations and welfare-work is too common now to be worth a "story" in any publication above the grade of house-organ. The big chiefs have men to write speeches for them, men to interpret news for them, men to study problems for them. Otherwise, they would never get their work done, for all their high speed and long hours.

United States Steel is one of our modern dukedoms, with holdings in many states and foreign climes, with vessels and railroads at command, with an army of stockholders and a still vaster army of workmen. Ford heads another, and in some ways an even more interesting one, because it has grown up under our eyes in a single generation and is even yet merely the definitely prolonged shadow of an original personality, with a desire to humanize industrial relations.

Just as the feudal leader who captured the imagination of his followers became the object of a hero-myth, so the Ford myth may be discerned cumulating to-day. The mystic strain in the man draws heavily upon the mysticism of the masses. He is the wonder-worker; at his edict wages rise, and defunct railroads earn dividends. Able, he must be; and yet he rose on favoring circumstances, and more than once has been saved by the inexorable operations of economic causes which he gives no hint of comprehending. But there is no use citing those causes to a Ford enthusiast; the Ford myth is already too strong. Some day it may be as hard to discover the cold truth about Ford as it is about Cromwell, Napoleon, or Washington. The Roosevelt myth is already set, adamant and indestructible; the Ford myth is still growing, gaining strength and depth day by day. Well, we cannot escape our myths and must live with them, for better or worse. The point is that, since myths accumulate around none other than socially significant persons, the Ford myth validates Ford as socially significant in the court of last resort — the soul of the masses.

The significance of industrial leaders in our days may be measured almost mathematically. When a smith employing two helpers bargained with the third, the newcomer was one fourth as significant as the boss. When the boss has 20,000 men under him, then the man on the outside, looking in for a job, is only 1/20002 as significant as the other, and the boss, for practical purposes, bulks as large in the community as 20,000 helpers. Probably more, because, the more power is concentrated, the deeper it cuts through the social strata.

How significant an industrial leader can be to a town is brought forcibly home by a sudden shift in the succession of grand dukes in our town. The former incumbent, whose industries employed 25,000 of our

100,000 population, was a native son, who started on a shoestring and went far enough to be deposed in Wall Street. He was a mighty seller of goods, not primarily a financier; and, in order to have goods to sell, he built, it seems, somewhat too fast and furiously. In building factories he also built a city — 13000, to 100,000, in twenty years.

Ten years ago or so he left us for New York, thereby becoming an absentee duke; but occasionally he returned on flying trips, which were duly noted in the public prints for our guidance and satisfaction. Even *in absentia*, however, he remained our leading citizen. We leaned upon him in ways that must have tried his patience. We could get no highly important public enterprise under way until he had given it his sanction by telegraph or messenger. Ever and anon we held him up for money. His name was on our lips oftener than that of any president except Roosevelt. So he was our hero, actual at the start, mythical toward the end — almost our god. In fact, I fancy some of our real-estate men prayed to him o' nights, since he so clearly possessed the power to make or break them. All the young fellows admired him, because he was doing precisely what they would have liked to do if they could; the elders were grateful to him for boosting the value of their holdings. Even those too conservative to buy his stocks found their realty values soaring as he built. He was our bridge to fortune; we relied upon him for prosperity, and usually got it with little trouble. Our local autocrat was Billy, yet he graciously kept the velvet glove over the iron hand,

and preferred to stand among us rather as first among equals.

In return, we gave him loyalty, and as little bother as a pioneer engaged in large-scale operations could expect. Labor troubles were rare. His old workmen knew him, and talked about him to the new ones. All were aware that he played baseball as a kid, sold fire insurance as a youth, and battled through to the top by himself. All agreed that he was generous and democratic, called folks by their first names, and was not above darting into a quick lunch for a sandwich. Our newspapers never missed an opportunity to praise at once his eminence and his commonplaceness. Labor was for him on two counts: first, he paid high wages and never cut them; second, he did not fit in neatly with the Wall Street scheme of things. Wages were cut when he was out of the saddle and Wall Street in the saddle; *ergo*, Billy was the friend of the boys, and Wall Street their enemy. As a matter of fact, perhaps, if costs had been watched acutely, there would have been no need to go to Wall Street for funds. But that question need not enter here.

Now the "boys" have a new boss, whom they have never seen, and they have taken a wage-cut. The morale in the factories is low; the men are working efficiently with "the fear of God" in their hearts. But the fear is not so much of God as of the Big Stick. Loyalty has worn thin; their hero has departed; the rank and file have lost their comforting myth and face stark reality. They speak of the notable American family now in control, and with a century-old record of fair dealing with labor, as "them Jews from Wall Street." These new bosses they have never seen, and they have no conception of them as other than a power over their lives, a far-away, intangible power, impersonal almost as the Deity. The men, as I write, are sore, feeling themselves caught and about to be sacrificed to a money Moloch. This may be, I think it is, nonsense; but it is mental poison to Tom, Dick, and Harry; and time — the sovereign antidote — will be required to disillusion them. Another myth must grow up around the central figure in their work-relations before they can forget Duke Billy, and follow confidently their new leader.

It has become rather the fashion for our modern dukes to leave their plants to assistants, and take themselves off to New York, where they pay court to King Capital as assiduously as the dukes of France courted the Bourbons. There must be some economic advantage in this hegira; but there certainly are disadvantages. This is the last step in the separation of the man and his boss in sympathies, in mutual responsibilities as citizens in the community. Even Billy was growing away from us toward the end; a less imaginative man would have done so long before.

The simple lives of workingmen, their hard-won homes and brave efforts to maintain the American standard of living in those homes — these ought to be under the eyes of their real boss most of the time. Statements of accountants, earnings-sheets and cost-records, show less than the great employer needs to know. The best welfare-work many a corporation chief could do would be to come home and take a personal interest in the human problems of his factory. But where the big boss has a dozen, or two dozen, plants in his string, what then? The evil holds; the remedy is not so apparent.

This brings us face to face with one of the puzzles of the Industrial Age. How far can concentration of industry go? Has it reached its limits? No categorical answer is possible; but the evidence leans toward the affirmative.

While the law may set temporary limits upon combinations, economics has the last word. Business is personality applied to the satisfaction of material wants through coöperating humans. The coöperating group which the leader captains is likely to be a measure of his ability to lead, since the group will not long remain efficient beyond the limits of his authority. If the big boss cannot bring his will to bear upon the furthest-removed laborer in the company's furthest-removed mill, then the corporation is too large to function economically under him. Competition will enforce one of two changes — either the group will be reduced in size to the point where the management functions efficiently, or a new manager must be sought. If a new manager cannot be found, efficient enough to cope with the extended problem, the group proceeds toward dissolution, usually not in one slide into bankruptcy, but by a gradual descent, interrupted by stages where things are held steady by efficient management. At any of these stages, however, the problem is precisely the same as it was at the beginning; if the manager is bigger than his job, the concern can grow up to the limit of governing circumstances; otherwise, it will take another slide. The decline of a corporation, like the decline of a state, — the Roman Empire, for example, — is marked by a feverish search for leaders, and by stages of advance or retreat, according as those leaders meet effectively the circumstances confronting them.

The extent to which industry may be concentrated, therefore, depends upon two factors: the personal force behind the decision, and the receptivity of labor to that thought-transference. The further away labor stands from the real boss, in space, ideals, habit of thought, and manner of life, the more difficult it becomes to maintain authority in toil, side by side with democracy in politics. Since, in a pinch between the two, the latter may be considered the stronger and more enduring, the tendency of the future, in theory, must be toward smaller units rather than larger, unless some unforeseen improvement in communication is effected. Practically, of course, the amelioration of present-day discontent by compromises toward coöperation may check the theoretical tendency; and it is even possible that, as industry advances toward more complete coöperation, still larger units may be agglomerated under one head. But that will merely be the substitution of a mental getting-together for the physical getting-together which meant so much to labor in the old days, and the loss of which now distresses the laborer. Needless to say, the path toward this mental *rapprochement* is roundabout and difficult, as compared with the direct short cut of the boss on the job; and it may not be worth the effort, when the man behind the pay-roll can come home and get on the big end of his job — work-relations. Finance is a necessary evil; speculation an unnecessary evil — work is neither, and must be served.

From not more than twenty per cent of the population is drawn the industrial aristocracy whose tenure of power rests absolutely upon their ability to think and do. That group contains those who have risen from the ranks, as well as those coming, ready financed, to the seats of the mighty. But it is worthy of note that, while inherited wealth may place a man aloft, it cannot guarantee his continuing in authority. There is always room at the top, because the mortality rate in industrial leadership is so high. One stumble, and the victim usually may as well hand in his resignation. If he is too firmly fixed in his seat for quick removal, competition whittles away at the foundation of his structure. Make good or go down — that is the iron law of industry.

There is this ever-present social danger in competition — that it drives men to decisions oftentimes harsher than they would make if they were not under its pressure. To preserve his group-organization — his corporation — solvent and efficient must ever be the chief concern of the industrial leader. Competition may not always give him time to work out plans fruiting far away; the financial situation may force him to adopt a harsh course with labor to-day, for instance, when he knows full well that, in the long run, a more considerate policy would be beneficial. Generally speaking, the man of ideals in industry finds play for his idealism in proportion as his enterprise is comfortably financed; when capital — the power to wait — gives him a chance to take at leisure hurdles which less-well-financed concerns must take in a rush. The better his position, the stronger he is for the long run.

A noteworthy example is that of Judge Gary in declining to cut wages as swiftly as minor concerns did, either through necessity or choice. The so-called soullessness of corporations is subject to this qualification: in so far as money and prevision can compensate for the human touch, the larger the business, the fairer are its practices. Here, again, the reaction of the corporation to ethics in trade and employment is largely the reaction of its leader. Big business cannot afford to be mean and small; its shop policy must be as straight as its market policy; and where either is crooked, the fault lies usually with a subordinate or distributor, who has played the company false. I refer here to conscious crookedness, and not to injustices which sometimes flow from mistaken policies applied with overbearing weight.

How to keep competition on a plane where enterprisers ethically inclined can satisfy labor, their stockholders, and the market is a chief concern of the public in our day. Cheap goods are a boon; but if competition toward cheapness grinds labor down in morale and buying power, the worth-whileness of cheap goods vanishes into thin air. We heard much, some years ago, about fair competition, which was interpreted to mean the restricting of competition to a point where small-scale operators could continue production when opposed by large-scale operators. There is, of course, much to be said for that; but, on the other hand, there would equally be something to be said on the advisability of protecting large-scale enterprises, with liberal labor policies, against small-scale competitors, whose labor-code is more primitive. Certainly the ethics of employment — an advancing code, upon which I pin more faith than upon any other factor for the unraveling of the tangle of interests and instincts into which the common use of automatic machinery has brought modern society — scarcely can reach fruition in an absolutely free and open field, where the least ethical travel light, and the more ethical are under self-imposed weights. Yet dynamic forces cannot be standardized. Associations of producers may go some distance in relieving this situation. Public opinion, perhaps, may do more by supporting the citizen-boss and frowning upon the miser-boss. If these do not serve, then the state doubtless will try its hand — whether for good or evil, none may say in advance of trial.

For the state must reckon with the men who boss automatic machinery, whose commands bring forth new machines and shift populations, whose success fills the coffers of the Federal treasury with taxes, whose exports create trade-balances, and whose imports create treasury-balances. If the state had no concern for the common man in his wrestling with the Iron Man, if the state were pure capitalist, it still would have to reckon with the uncommon man in the industrial saddle. But a state tinged ever so little with democracy, even faintly conscious of its responsibilities to the mass, must consider how the mass fares under its bosses while operating these new tools. In this America of ours, founded in revolt and geared to universal suffrage, there is no dodging that issue, even for an instant.

Our industrial leaders, rather than the statesmen and educators, carry the destinies of modern America on their shoulders. They are doing some very wonderful things, some of which they but dimly apprehend. At the same time that they are raising the standard of living, they are contributing to a solidarity of labor and a mediocrity of type hitherto unknown in America. Variations of earning power and social position, based on craft-skill, are disappearing from our world. Rural and town labor are fusing in ideas as in function. Our ablest minds set the public a pace so fast that weak spots are uncovered in the mental armor of less competent individuals, a process tending toward lower levels in the plebs.

But perhaps the most important thing that they are doing, of which they are not altogether conscious, appears on the credit side of the ledger. They are training the workaday world in coöperation. No such school of coöperation in mundane affairs has ever been set up as that operated for profit by American corporations. With every improvement in process and every expansion of scope, the day is brought nearer when the lesson shall have been learned and the attempt to apply it made.

Whether the attempt to amend the basis of industrial coöperation in the popular interest shall succeed, depends in large measure on the orientation which our driving men of affairs make in the face of the growing demand by the workers for a larger share in shaping their own destinies. As I see the situation, the attempt will fail unless practical, experienced minds give it direction and leadership. We shall have exactly as much, perhaps more, need for industrial leaders then, need for their adaptability, their determination; and we shall have to make such terms with them as will keep them in the game, or else let civilization slump. The trend toward coöperation proceeds with infinite variety of adjustments between dynamic forces, and must go forward in that way; standardization would be fatal to our whole order.

But the impulse toward coöperation is strong and determining — one of those popular, settled mandates before which the few must bow or yield. The few can best serve society and themselves by yielding gracefully but not too soon; seeking always to preserve the identity of their groups; building upon the public service which those groups indubitably perform, and trusting the public to recognize that service in due time; contenting themselves with the social by-products of power — eminence, public regard, and clear consciences — in lieu of the baser satisfactions which minister to individual wants and vanities.

V

INDUSTRY AND THE STATE

SPEAKING of John Marshall, former Senator Beveridge says: "He was a true gentleman, in that he respected the personalities of others, even of the humblest." The Iron Man, from this standpoint, is no gentleman, since his invasion of personality is instant and ruthless. Men schooled in independence and fed high on the truths, half-truths, and fallacies of democracy, resent this invasion instinctively, though they may be brought by training and experience to accommodate themselves to it. Necessity forces a compromise with the feelings, and habit comes to their rescue; nevertheless, millions of self-assertive egos struggle every hour of our days and nights against the monotony and subordination involved in the "vast, repetitive processes" of modern industry. The defective may not be irked by the grind, the effective may be roused to enthusiasm by opportunities which automatic machinery and interchangeable manufacture offer to his ambitions; but the mass lying between these upper and nether layers of the social cake is neither content nor thrilled. Hence the widespread fretfulness which we call social unrest.

The articulate note of this unrest, and its chief political aspect, is resentment against owners and managers of machines, against capitalists, bosses, and proprietors. It has many catch-phrases, of which "industrial democracy" is just now the most meaningful. In deference to this outcry from the mass, legislatures here and abroad have busied themselves for many years in passing laws in control of work-relations and abridging individual liberty in the use and disposition of property. A goodly share of current legislation is of this regulatory character; and of late we have seen an extension of this influence in the granting to certain groups of citizens — notably to farmers organized into coöperative societies and laborers organized into unions — of a license to do what groups of managers and proprietors may not do. Nevertheless, unrest continues, and more persons listen daily without protest to proposals that the institution of private property either be destroyed, root and branch, or at least excluded from control over all socially necessary forms of wealth.

Champions of these extremist proposals have not overlooked the asocial and anti-social effects of growing automatization. They consider that the increasing use of automatic machinery under private ownership presents to society and the state the evils of industrial capitalism in such concentrated form, that the proletariat must come into control of the machines, or descend into a new slavery. Industry, they say, is not worth preserving unless socialized. Socialists would effect this through the state; Communists through group administration of property held and worked in common — a modern adaptation of the ancient commune. Anarchists prefer a governorless society, in which the nice adjustments of modern industry, based as they are on enforceable contracts,

could not be maintained. Inside these major alignments are many divisions, which so far weaken the
practical politics of the opposition that the institution
of private property, firmly rooted in the instincts,
continues to function in countries nominally Socialist,
and to gain strength month by month even in Communist Russia.

Observing labor's dissatisfaction to be increasing,
despite increased reward and higher standards of living, it is inevitable that men take to explaining
radicalism in non-economic terms. One says "work-
neurosis"; another, "overstimulation of modern life";
still another, Stewart Paton of Princeton, stresses
"the defense reactions of inadequates." Granting a
measure of truth to each diagnosis, no single one is
altogether satisfactory; and, even lumped together,
they do not quite satisfy. To say that individuals sufficient to influence social judgments are inadequate
to meet their personal problems competently, is quite
as severe a judgment upon the civilization presenting
those problems to frail humanity as it is upon frail
humans for being downhearted in their presence.
When a system of living becomes too complex for the
common man of good-will to adjust himself thereto
with reasonable comfort and confidence, the inade-
quacy is the system's, not the individual's. Life and
human nature are primary; civilization and industry
are secondary to them, and cannot be maintained
unamended much longer than the masses find them
worth while. He who forgets this elemental fact builds
his theories upon the sand; the state which does not

reckon with it at every turn is preparing for revolution.

Regulation of industrial processes by the state in the interest of society, therefore, is sound in principle, however ill devised its regulating ordinances may be, however cumbersome and wasteful its administrative processes. States may not be proceeding by the most direct routes to correct the social weaknesses which modern industry develops; but the people surely have shown common sense in insisting that each state attend to the situation as best it can before the case gets out of hand. Perceiving the foundations of society to be shaken by the competitive strivings of our effectives, the potency of machine industry to breed war, shift populations, cause the race to degenerate, and rob life of many of its humbler compensations, our people would ill deserve their political heritage did they not strive, however blindly, to correct the balance by calling in their sovereign ally — the state. The call has been sounded and heard. The state may have fumbled; nevertheless, it has moved. To-day the danger is not so much that the state may lag, as that it may move too fast and too far, shifting over from a reasonable control, in which innovators may work out their ideas without substantial distress to the public, to arbitrary direction under which bureaucracy stifles individual initiative and autocracy nullifies group-decisions.

There is apparent in the civilized world to-day a drift toward state control of industry, so marked that it may bring us shortly to a conscious revival of "state mercantilism." Read out of court long since by Adam Smith in his "Wealth of Nations," political manipulation of trade draws renewed strength from a number of sources. Foremost, of course, is this defensive reaction, wide and strong, by the people against submergence in automatism. Coal-and-iron states depend for solvency more than ever upon business earnings. Nationals expect their states to protect their overseas profits and investments, from which develops the corollary that states must guard against possible consequences by approving overseas economic adventures in advance. Political invasion of business, breaking down easily into class and special legislation, offers unusual opportunities to politicians to expand their influence and emoluments, and is as water on the wheels of bureaucracies keen to perpetuate themselves. Improvements in transportation and communication now make comparatively easy intense economic unity in even the largest of industrial states. Their governments, too, are moving consciously to alleviate domestic unrest and build up nationalist strength, by assisting their nationals to export goods and import raw materials on favorable terms, to the end that jobs may be plenty and questions few.

Many lesser considerations might be listed, among them the witless habit of the press in forever calling upon the state to do something about something, usually something which the press soon will have forgotten and later shall regret. The result of all these forces is a steady drift toward popular acceptance of the state as a sovereign economic as well as a sovereign political unit; but here again the pragmatist in politics perceives the danger as one of excess rather than of direction.

Before establishing the state as the everyday dictator of business, before advancing the statesman from the rôle of referee to that of manager, it is well to consider gravely the character and limitations of the state and its animators. The people, feeding on phrases, take as inspired revelation too much claptrap. It is high time to discuss in terms of reality institutions usually dismissed in shibboleths. The words "industrial democracy" stand out nobly by themselves; but it is worth pondering whether, in practice, industrial democracy would not degenerate, as political democracy has degenerated, into a mazy intrigue of wordy place-hunting and piffling conferences, in which facile chaps who will promise anything too often outstrip blunt men who can promise nothing. A political democracy so poisoned and ensnared may be borne with, in spite of its disabilities, for the sake of its past and for the faith in its future. But to make and sell goods on that basis would be as impossible as for Uncle Sam to lift himself by his boot-straps. A strong commercial nation can carry poor government a long way without breaking; yet the most efficient government so far organized by man would be helpless in the industrial complex that free peoples have developed through bargaining.

To admit the practical limitations of state sovereignty is exactly as important as admitting the state's vital interest in just work-relations. By common consent we accept the sovereignty of the state, for the sake of tranquillity at home and safety abroad. Those powers which, in private hands, lead to the oppression of the many by the few, — the right to make and enforce laws, to maintain armed forces, make war, levy customs and taxes, — these inhere in the state as we know it. Yet the truth is that these sovereign powers are the result of growth, accretion, conquest, and are maintained only by ceaseless vigilance. The state, here and there, is even now extending its dominion over education to include supervision over private educational institutions. And it seems likely that, presently, it will have to resist the invasion of its monopoly over armed forces by declaring against the growing tendency of corporations to rely for property protection upon companies of private guards, a practice common in sparsely settled sections and often producing grave results, as in West Virginia of late. Broadly speaking, whatever power the state may gain is never yielded except on compulsion or through negligence. Revolution — active or passive — is the only certain means by which the governed can recover valid freedom of action in lines over which the state has assumed sovereignty. This fact alone ought to be enough to give us pause in the process of expanding sovereign powers over business. To yield rights is easier far than to regain them. Those liberties for work and trade, which we enjoy so carelessly and seem to value so lightly, were wrung from states by men who knew the oppressions of state management, and esteemed such rights the essence of freedom. To surrender them at whim, or fired by ideas which time is likely to prove fallacious, is absurdly imprudent.

Theoretically, the state can commandeer the persons and properties of its citizens; actually, the process is difficult, except when the nation is one with the state in purpose. But the state's empire ends with tangibles; it cannot coerce the intangibles; cannot summon talents and loyalties by fiat. At every point in its progress, the state wins and holds loyalty only by conferring benefits, real or fancied; and upon penalty of utter stagnation, it must give talent elbow-room.

Political history reveals a never-ending conflict between the mass and the class for the control of the state's political machinery. In a democracy the conflict may be considered as resolved in favor of the mass, in theory, if not always in practice. The very existence of the state is, indeed, a triumph for the common man; the institution is his champion against defective and effective alike; the state is his, and he made it in his own image.

Deep in his heart the common man is conservative. Social revolutions are begun by extraordinary men of Utopian vision; but after a while, the cloud-compellers must come down to earth and make good a programme of simplification. Usually they move too slowly toward moderation to satisfy the people, and so lose their heads along with their leadership. The French Revolution erected a state which was to enforce Liberty, Equality, and Fraternity, and ended in enforcing peasant-proprietorship. Russia is headed in the same direction; the Bolshevist swing from left to right is in the nature of things. The complications of the Communist régime have bitterly disappointed the peasantry, who thought life under the Empire and in the Mir already too complicated, and fancied that life might be simpler with those institutions abolished. Madero talked the Brotherhood of Man to his Mexicans for years; but not until he promised them "forty acres and a mule" did his campaign sweep the country. Indeed, the equivalent of forty acres and a mule — security and independence made certain in some time-honored, clearly understood way — is precisely what the common man needs and wants. Our radicals of to-day play, consequently, upon a resentment conservative at base — the distress of simple natures at impacts of forces beyond their ken; the hankering of the many to get back to a scheme of life in which they can be more self-reliant and lean less upon factors beyond their control.

Too much emphasis has been given, I think, to the hypothetical quarrel over the division of profits, as an incentive to social unrest. That has its influence, of course; but too much can be made of it. Our common man, now as ever, expects from life little more than a living — sensible view, since that is all he gets, and probably all he ever can get. His chief quarrel lies, I think, not with the pay, but with the work and the conditions under which it goes forward. Above all else, he prefers to earn his living in old, tried ways, without too much fretting and shifting. He resents change; his chief grudge against his leaders and masters of to-day is that they will not let him alone, to do as his fathers did before him, to do now as he himself did ten years ago.   Left to himself, he would have settled with the machine at its birth — by torch and axe.

Progress may deliver physical comfort and convenience; but to minds essentially static, these boons may be bought at too much of mental discomfort and inconvenience. Progress involves insecurity along with change; since security is a primal need of his nature, the common man is bound to doubt the desirability of progress. He has succeeded in passing this doubt along to the state to this extent, that the state stands first of all for security, and is suspicious of novelty. The state is a reservoir, sometimes stale and foul, of tradition and precedent, a bulwark of order and mediocrity, and the most static thing in a changing universe, except its former team-mate — the church. The very name — the state — implies no change; a misnomer, perhaps, yet significant as expressing the mass ideal of security.

The sovereign state represents the common sense of common folk. "Better one master than many," say the people, ever and ever, after trying the many; "better even tyranny than oligarchy; better to be chained to an immovable post than batted through life by irresistible forces." So the masses have decided time and again, and must ever decide when the issue is drawn between institutionalized and personalized power. Their decisions, in the past, have seldom been articulate; but their acquiescence comes down to the same thing. The strong can protect themselves; they have no need of law, while the weak need it every hour.

Political action, then, is the answer of those who plod to those who leap. Through statutes and courts are expressed, in due course, verdicts enforceable because approved by settled public opinion. In the very nature of the state itself, the sovereign verdict is normally negative. "Thus far and no farther," says the state to these gifted individuals who, singly or in groups, and answering egoistic urges, would drive the masses ahead of them, in order to satisfy measurably their personal instincts toward dominance. In emergencies the state assumes positive direction, and speaks in the affirmative, saying, "Go and do," instead of the usual "Halt and do not." But for a democracy this right-about-face is a forced putt, and wearies folk who fret under compulsion in any form, and resent it all the more in unaccustomed forms. Democratic governments take the initiative at their peril: *vide* our mid-war elections. Even an autocratic state plays with fire when it marshals economic forces and attempts to direct progress; soon it must return to its static ideal, perhaps to dry-rot the faster for the lianas of red tape generated in its enforced activity.

In proportion as our government departs from reasonable control of individual and group efforts, it vitiates its constitutional principles and slides toward autocracy, no less autocratic because power may have shifted from rich to poor, from informed to ig-

norant. Moreover, democracy never creates: men—
gifted individuals — plunge out of the mass, to create,
in the sight of their less gifted but envious fellows,
those ameliorations of life which, in their complex and
imperfect workings, constitute civilization. Consequently, control, and not direction of personal and
group efforts, is and should remain the accredited
means of protecting our society from becoming the
pawns of its industrial leaders. Other peoples, less
individualist in tradition and with less to lose, may go
further; but for us the losses involved in state-led
industry must far exceed the gains.

There was a time when this conflict between mass
and class, between mediocrity and ability, between
the state and outstanding individuals, was complicated by the overshadowing tradition of the Rights of
Man — certain inalienable rights, vested in each of
us by mere accident of birth. Fortunately, these need
not becloud the present situation. When business
leaders of a century or more ago, seeking limitation
of risk, struck that bargain with the State of New
York, resulting in the first general incorporation law
(1811), they exchanged a measure of commercial liberty for a measure of legal protection. Now that
business functions almost entirely through corporations, the state's ultimate authority over business
stands undebatable. The state charters the corporation; licenses it to live so many years, for purposes of
profit, in the doing of this or the holding of that. The
created never can rise superior to its creator. No
matter how great a corporation — or the whole net-

work of corporations — grows, the masterful business *bloc*, a genuine community in thought if not *in loco*, never can dodge the dour truth that there is a greater than itself — the state.

Furthermore, the business *bloc* must realize that the state acts, ultimately, upon the mandate of the people. The state, on receipt of that mandate may delay, consult its beloved precedents, mark time to escape the possible errors of snap judgment, and to give counter-propaganda a hearing; but if popular pressure be maintained, eventually it must act as directed, on penalty of revolution. Even so conservative a body as the Supreme Court discovers that it is possible to change opinions from one decade to another, without bringing the Constitution down in ruins; indeed, if the masses remain insistent, a quiet mental revolution in high places is the approved method of averting a noisy physical revolution in the streets.

"The great cause of revolution," according to Macaulay, "is this, that while nations move onward, constitutions stand still." Yes, but interpretation is a buffer absorbing many shocks; the legal mind, pressed hard enough, discovers divers ways of letting "freedom broaden slowly down from precedent to precedent," that would astonish the Fathers. Call up all the traditions you please; they have but advisory, not primary, value. The adjustment between the state and the corporation proceeds, therefore, on the basis of expediency. The people, through their coercive agent, — the state, — will go as far as need be to protect their primary interests; and stop, presumably,

only when convinced that nothing can be gained by
going further.

In other times and places states have fought their
aspiring individuals on battlefields and battlements;
now the state proceeds in law and courts and legislatures, though none the less vital for all its peaceful
setting. Two projections of Man's imaginative faculty grapple there with one another. Neither was in
the beginning, yet it is impossible for most of us to
imagine the end of either. They are will-associations,
become so natural to us that life without them would
be chaos. Yet even in their most desperate clinches,
the animating minds behind each are aware that each
is essential to the other, and that, were one to fall, the
other must be dragged in its train. So they face each
other, mutually distrustful, mutually dependent, like
Siamese twins, who never agree completely, yet must
agree somewhat to get anywhere.

On the one side is the highest expression of the social will, the state, captained by two sorts of men —
able tribunes and mouthy demagogues, and manned by
bureaucrats fatuously obsessed, for the most part, by
the *status quo*. On the other side are ranged lusty,
virile children of their stodgy sire — business organizations in which many persons, following the universal instinct to get the most at the least effort, cohere
under the leadership of gifted individuals spurred to
achievement by overmastering instincts toward dominance. One, the apotheosis of political genius, fixed,
august — a unity; the other a coherence of economic
genius, ganglion of many groups, each highly adapt-

able. The latter capable of doing anything well, provided there is money in it, and few questions asked; applying boldly what power it has, and avid for more; the former fumbling over tasks that its servants ought to know well; yet scrupulous to a hair, and chary of exercising its full powers except in emergencies.

The state is a conscience, slow, majestic, just, more concerned with principles than returns, with methods than results; the corporation is a will, effective, shrewd, justifying means by ends, born to make money by getting things done, and impatient at whatever baulks the fulfillment of that destiny. The one is static, cleaving to precedent, cherishing tradition and gratefully adopting new myths, as such spring from the incurable mysticism of the masses. The other is dynamic, blind to the past, keen toward the future, ignoring costs which do not show on the ledger, and prone to pass along those costs—among which are the asocial and anti-social effects of automatic machinery — to the state for settlement.

This is merely a new phrasing of a problem old as history, — in fact, the key-problem of civilization, — how shall the mass preserve its rights and grow in the fullness thereof, and yet give dominant individuals enough leeway to contribute to life ameliorations which they alone can give in abundance, contributions which eventually become part of the social heritage? In a democracy whose founders bargained in council to establish the state, and for a people who live by bringing things to market almost entirely upon the basis of the bargain, this is the root-bargain of all.

How the bargain is struck, what are its terms and implications, and how it is enforced and amended — in these terms may nations be interpreted, as they move toward unity or dissolution.

France, through the Middle Ages, relieved her nobles of power and left them their privileges. The monarchy became absolute, the nobles, courtiers; and Louis XIV could say with truth, "I am the state." Descendants of great captains, local leaders who had kept provinces and populations in line for the state, degenerated into puppets. Since the state did everything, they had nothing left to do; and presently were able to do nothing more meaningful than watch Louis don his shirt. When a smile from the King's mistress came to mean more than famine in their titular domains, revolution waited just around the corner. Then, when the monarchy had sore need of men to plan, to organize, to fight, these tissue-leaders had nothing with which to brace the state which had sucked away their birthrights — neither wills, nor funds, nor men-at-arms.

Political development in Germany took another tack. Lacking a stay-at-home overlord, the emperors being off at wars beyond the Alps, the German dukes retained both power and privileges. Hundreds of political subdivisions, yeasty bubblings of sovereignty many of them, made mediæval Germany a checkered cockpit, alike for civil and foreign wars. Thus the unifying of Germany was delayed until 1870, a chronic belligerency strangling parliamentary politics and inuring anciently free peoples to autocratic rule.

The English, folk of give-and-take, followed the middle course in this respect, as otherwise. They refused their aristocracy privileges, but left them power — political and economic power, rooted in land ownership. Commons, expressing the common sense of the public, played King against nobles, and *vice versa*, backing the King when the nobles bore down too severely, backing the nobles when the monarchy leaned toward despotism and the destruction of olden liberties. Thus, when kings fell, as fall they did, there remained dukes and earls and squires, strong in will and purpose, to administer the government. 'T is said the English love a lord; well, they may, considering the services of so many of them. Holding firmly to its power to tax, which was based on faith that the people would pay tax-moneys only as it decreed, the Commons came forward, clinging now to the royal vestments, now to the stirrups of the aristocrats, until such time as it could dominate the realm. Long ago it reduced the King to a functionary, a personalization of the state, a regal rubber-stamp. And finally, by threatening to apply this rubber-stamp on sufficient warrants of nobility, it reduced the House of Lords to minor status by breaking its power of absolute veto. Whether this act in the political drama of the Empire be good or ill, the method of democratic infiltration which accomplished it must be rated successful, since it bridged the gap from feudalism to popular government without a destructive revolution, giving Britain world-leadership while France was still in chaos, and Germany as yet merely a geographical description.

Industrially England followed the same course. From 1765, when inventions for applying steam-power to manufacture gave the factory system firm footing, down to the Reform Bill of 1832, British enterprisers had a free hand. They originated, organized, and directed, harnessed natural forces, built new towns and merchant fleets, sent their goods across the seas, made London the centre of world-trade and finance, and took toll from the labors and resources of the whole planet, bringing in abundant wealth upon which the state levied taxes. Their enterprises forced government, often dilatory and unwilling, to regularize unbecoming situations overseas by hoisting the royal standard, where the Union Jack first appeared for "business as usual."

As might have been expected, evils appeared coincidentally with benefits. Comparatively free of state-control, masters, in competition with one another, followed their inclinations too far for the common good. Labor cowered under brutal laws in restraint of combinations for wage-bargaining. Working conditions so vile that none but a virile race could have survived them obtained side by side with a standard of living crowded down toward the starvation-point. Actually, there were years when British labor earned less than a living, though working long hours, the difference being made up in poor relief. The class refused to pay the mass living wages, but consented, quixotically, to be taxed for the difference between real wages and living wages. To read this record (John L. and Barbara Hammond: "The Village Labourer";

"The Town Labourer") is to shudder at what industrial leaders will do in competition with one another, when the state remains deaf to the travail of the masses. Given equal opportunity, I fancy our enterprisers would do as ill, not because they are wicked, but because they are intensely human, and discovering moral justifications for whatever leads to one's power and prosperity is as instinctive as the desire to gain those boons.

Rather than countenance the faintest return to such mass misery, I would agree to the state's clipping the wings of industrial genius afresh each morning. Yet, after all, these same builders of British industry, in their struggle with the landlords, secured the enfranchisement of their workingmen; whereupon the latter, in due course, undertook the protection of their work-interests through organization and of their social interests through legislation. The liberalizing of the British political system was in large part a by-product of the self-seeking of British industrialists. Also, these leaders, in return for nothing more tangible than freedom to trade, and paying taxes the while, contributed more to the state in territory, wealth, and prestige than the state could have secured by exercising all its sovereign powers in the most arbitrary fashion. Measured merely by the yardstick of service to the state, and to the hitherto unenfranchised masses, their contribution is incredibly vast and valuable, in spite of the miseries incident to its inception and growth. No Briton lives to-day who is not to some extent the heir of the labors of those industrial leaders

and especially of the early innovators of machine-tools
— Watt, Wilkinson, Bramah, Maudslay, Brunel,
Clement, Whitworth, and the rest.

This brief hark-back to the infancy of the industrial
system indicates what a state's creative citizens can
do, both for evil and for good, when permitted to follow the main chance full-tilt to any lengths. Their
social contributions, though usually by-products, are
none the less invaluable to peoples adaptable enough
to withstand the strain of progress. James J. Hill
built his railroads, not to serve the state, but to serve
his Ego. He kept at it long after he might have retired, a made man, because railroad-building had become his medium of self-expression. As an artist loves
to put oil and color on canvas for the good of his soul,
so Hill loved to conquer space with steel; perhaps also
he cherished the adulation which comes to a picked
man after he picks himself and proves the wisdom of
his choice. But the fact is that, whatever Jim Hill
thought or willed in the matter, actually he served the
state and society, and his by-product of service ex-
ceeds what the state would have wrung from him as
direct product under duress. Indeed, in a state which
built its own railroads, Hill must have died a village
teamster; his type prefers to run peanut-stands "on
its own" than to go through the palavering incident
to getting things done through government. And
while we may always pay the Hill heirs hire for that
service, capitalized full well, still the Northwest is sure
to think well enough of its bargain to teach in its public schools the parenthood of its railroads.

Effectives like Hill possess in a superlative degree survival value; they live in works which pass into public possession, either in fee simple or for use at rates which the state sees to it, soon or late, are reasonable. To deny such individuals reasonable scope for action is to impoverish posterity. There are not too many of them. At heart we know them to be our dear ones, doing that which each of us would do if he could; we must be choice of them, for our own sake and that of our children; but — but — the eternal but — we must keep them from eating us up in the fascinating play of that mad game of theirs, in which they jostle one another for elbow-room, wealth, and eminence.

There is a good deal of nonsense talked by indignant business men these days which can be explained only by lack of background. Their chambers of commerce feed them with everything but that which they most need — philosophy. Yet amid so much smoke there must be some fire; and I think business men are justified in resenting the state's inability to approach them without suspicion, and with some appreciation of their services. Every corporation worthy of the name, whether it produces shoestrings or transportation, serves the public at the same time that it serves its stockholders. In so far as its goods or services ameliorate life, it contributes something to society which, rightly used, has ethical value. The motive of civilization is economic, but its goal is ethical. The industrial leader wants to be understood, wants credit for the ethical by-product of his economic efforts. But the state, with so many dry-as-dust officials watching

industry lest it slip, looks upon shoelaces and transportation alike as subject-matter for statistics first,
and taxation second. Instead of rating producers according to the justice of their labor policies, and their
fairness to customers, the state appears to judge them
by the completeness of their records; and the scarlet
corporate sin of the moment is to fail to supply quite
all the information that a bureau clerk needs, to keep
him busy the rest of his uneventful days.

This suspicious attitude is, perhaps, an inevitable
outcome of corrupt corporate practices. In the name
of business, practical men, esteeming themselves
pillars of the established order, have in the past sinned
grievously against the state and society. A few have
been caught and convicted; more have been held up to
shame in the public prints; but the majority, no doubt,
have escaped either fate, through insufficiency of laws,
venality of the courts and legislatures, the studied
indifference of the press, or the skill of their lawyers.
Their steals run the whole gamut of respectable vil-
lainy, from fraudulently sequestering the public domain to milking absentee stockholders through false
reports and cheating the public by combinations to
hold up prices. Books have been written about them,
and to the end of the chapter honest business must
suffer in fame and purse through these lapses from
common honesty and fair play.

It would be easy to write a sensational chapter on
the cheating of minority stockholders. So common is
such abuse of confidence that "blue-sky" legislation
is popular, on the theory that the money of the people

should be protected no less than the people themselves. Yet this corporate sabotage against capital in small lots is far less serious than other corporate evils of which the state takes little cognizance. Whoso buys common stock does so in expectation of profit, speculating for an uncertain income instead of investing for a settled one. His coöperation in the enterprise, therefore, is on quite another plane from that of the ordinary industrial worker, who must work or starve. The consuming public is in somewhat the same predicament, since the people must consume or perish. The establishment of work-standards and market-standards rests, therefore, upon the fundamental of protecting life and its amenities under pressure.

On the other hand, the common-stock holder enters and leaves the corporation at will, for profit only, and is not ill-used if required to take the bitter with the sweet. He cannot in fairness claim more protection for his speculative capital than is already his under the "false-pretense" section of the criminal code in most states, with rights of recovery, as established in civil law, for the safeguarding of minority stockholders. Since the state has every reason to promote investment and discourage speculation, state control of security issues should be concentrated upon establishing the soundness of fixed-interest issues. Meanwhile, through schooling and publicity, the sober economic truth should be drilled home, that he who buys common stock buys at his peril — the greater the return, the greater the risk. For the state to place any sort of protective covering over common-stock speculations, while savings banks, life insurance, and a well-filled bond market are open to the public, is unsound economically and politically.

At this pass, the finding of funds for industrial operations seems of prime importance; but as the co-operative spirit gains headway, industries are likely to draw less and less upon the public savings. Even now, the corporation whose machines are manned by operatives eager to produce worthy goods, whose employees hold no grudge, can finance itself abundantly through profits won fairly in free markets. Unfortunately, such corporations are few.

Between the corporation and capital exists no clash of wills, but merely a discrepancy of interest; the clash comes between many men and much capital. Capital and Labor stand on either side of a widening chasm, across which only the stronger laborers may leap, and across which men of good-will have increasing difficulty in making themselves heard. So the relation of the state to industry comes down, at the moment, to an issue of state-backed labor *versus* the corporations.

Thus far, state backing for labor has brought forth two sorts of government action — laws affecting all industrial labor (in the main beneficial), and laws and rulings affecting and benefiting only unionized labor. In steam-transportation the Federal government, heeding the loudest voice, accepted the brotherhoods so completely that the Pennsylvania's plan of employee representation is held unworkable by Mr. Atterbury, in the face of pro-union decisions by the Railway Labor Board.

In mill operations, however, craft-unionism is a dead issue, largely because of automatic machinery. There the gap must be bridged by employers dealing directly with their own men; otherwise, it will not be bridged at all. Consequently, the sooner the state ceases looking upon unionism as a panacea for all industrial labor ills, so much the better. The labor problem spreads far beyond union limits. The existence of the political *status quo* has come to depend upon the restoration of confidence between employer and employee. Exactly how it shall be restored, and through what media, is less important than the speed and completeness of its restoration. Those in command of large-scale industries are mostly committed to non-recognition of craft-unions, a policy based more upon instinct than upon reason, but, nevertheless, binding. They resent the intrusion of special pleaders from outside their industrial vale — a state of mind easy to understand in view of the sorry experience of managers in certain unionized lines of production, notably the building trades. However, many of the industrial leaders are moving directly toward a *rapprochement* with their employees, by various methods, all aimed at creating solidarity of the producing group as opposed to that craft-solidarity which is the union ideal. Statesmen might well consider whether, for industries localized and automatized, this development is not more logical and satisfactory than the other; and if so, devote more attention to hastening the process.

Obviously we are coming to perform, as large, co-ordinated groups, those economic life-processes which our ancestors performed singly, or by twos and threes. Whether this be good or ill is not determinable; the shift has its compensations as well as its difficulties. Mountainous as the latter seem at times, we are still far from having tried out all the controls, and are not likely to exchange our industrialized existence for something simpler until we arrive at our wits' ends. Thus far, political controls, forced upon business by the state as a penalty for past sins and protection against present puissance, have received far more attention than the efforts put forth by corporations to make industrial toil fit in with the physical, mental, and social well-being of their employees. Enlightened employers have been caught in the network of legislative inhibitions, along with the most benighted, notwithstanding the efforts of the former to undertake, at their own risk, betterments inuring to the comfort of the people and the safety of the state.

Obviously there is need here for discrimination; but, unfortunately, discrimination is not one of the state's strong points. The happiness of the mass is the state's ideal; but in a workaday world the state frequently stumbles, on its way thereto, over precedents, and its progress is woefully hampered by predilections toward order and uniformity. So far its servants seem unable to grasp the possibility of aiding mass happiness by giving men and corporations of good intent more leeway to extend experimentally the coöperative principle inherent in corporate operations, and already being pressed to good purpose by many business groups.

Yet the limitations of rigid political control of business, which tends inevitably toward state socialism, are so adamant to a people of our individualist heritage, and the freezing of our semi-fluid industrial society into class-conscious orders of employers and unionized workers seems so foreign to our traditions, that the state ought to make every possible concession to the principle of autonomous control before finally establishing its mastery, or clearing the way definitely for the Capital-Labor dog-fight sure to follow the intensification of class loyalties. To make the corporation, in which many already coöperate in the production and distribution of goods and earnings, a medium for the coöperative production and distribution of spiritual values as well, seems at all points the American way to harness the Iron Man to the common good, as automatization in industrial plants proceeds toward its predestined goal.

VI

THE CHANGING CORPORATION

THE Iron Man is owned by the corporation. One is as much an invention as the other; each represents an evolution, in which adaptations have been piled upon simple legal and mechanical principles. The automatic machine is as much a mechanical person as the corporation is a legal person. The two have long kept step with one another. Without the corporation to finance its development and distribute its produce, automatic machinery would still be in embryo — museum models instead of effective complexes grinding out goods, creating wealth and comforts, intensifying social and political problems. And without the Iron Man to make the ordinary run of humans useful in the production of intricate goods, corporations could not have reached their present proportions and influence. Automatic machinery is one of the forces establishing the truth of Lloyd's dictum, that "the natural person, as an enterpriser of consequence in industry, has ceased to exist."

Together, the corporation and the automatic machine form a team capable of prodigious feats of strength; but in their straightaway pull for profits, they plough a pitiless furrow through the crust of custom. Strong their drivers must be, and are; but the masses, paced by the machine in the shop and seldom outside the shop escaping from an environment motivated by industry, wonder if the controllers of their destinies are altogether to be trusted. And the analytic observer, too, must sometimes doubt whether even altruistic drivers may alter materially their course. Though vast ameliorations of life have flowed from this union, these have been by-products. A world grown more conscious of life-processes, a public seeking social welfare, waits to see if the corporation and the automatic machine can be swung somewhat away from private gain, and somewhat more toward public good.

The masses turn instinctively toward their champion—the sovereign state; laws in restraint of corporations multiply upon the statute books. The people are less aware than the politicians of the difficulty of applying political action to industrial ills. So the remote consequences of such application may be worse than the original infirmity. I recall that Governor Cummins converted the country to the "Iowa idea"; and I have lived to see Senator Cummins lead in returning the railroads to their owners on terms more expensive to the people than those in force when railroad-baiting began.

Since the state creates the corporation, one might infer complete mastery. Actually, the relationship is more that of a stout and querulous old mother to her lusty, ambitious sons. Corporations cannot be too closely bound to their parent without defeating the purposes of their creation. For one thing, the state cannot find elsewhere revenue so easily; the old woman calls upon her sons to bring taxes to her lap, and they come bearing, not only taxes, but other gifts also, strange gifts, things which the stout parent never dreamed of having — new fruits of faith and vision and toil which, in due time, become the accepted diet of a public forgetful of their origin. In this welter of novelty, the parent state clings stubbornly to traditions and principles; she may exult in the revenue her sons deliver and the gifts they bring: but her massive common sense enables her to see that such are of little worth if justice and mercy, and the common weal of her people, be sacrificed in the scramble for wealth and power. One can fancy her saying with a disconcerting naïveté:

"This is the stuff of life you bring me; but it is not life. I need these things; but, after all, they are not enough. I can't tell you just what to do, over and above bringing in my taxes; but I have no hesitancy in telling you what you may not do, as light comes to me. In order to keep you fit, I put you more or less on your honor; and I hope you will always behave better than I know how to make you behave. You move so fast, you really keep me quite fuddled; but every rule I lay down I mean for the best, anyway."

In the adjustment to be reached between public content and private interest, the most hopeful factor is the corporation. In itself a compromise between two instincts running constant in human nature, — the desire for gain and the desire for security, — the corporation is the instrument through which the socializing process now under way may work out most comfortably. It is a regulated vehicle of group-activity amenable to political control. Intangible and impersonal, existing only in the contemplation of the law, it possesses a superhuman virility, rising superior to death, accident, and many ills which beset frail humans. Given sound management and an acquiescent state, corporations may live forever. They partake to this extent of the static nature of the parent; yet are far more flexible in getting finite things done swiftly and cheaply. On the other hand, they are more dependable than individuals. They escape personal bias, wrath, prejudice, emotion; their nervous systems react keenly to but one set of stimuli — those of profit and loss. Still, they are not unresponsive to public opinion; and may perhaps be controlled more effectively thereby than by law. The public, you see, butters their bread.

One who puts forth the corporation as a means of grace champions an institution with abundant faults. Some of these inhere in the corporate form; others, the more evident and galling, are less serious because resulting from decisions of persons in corporate authority. The more important of these lapses may be dealt with under criminal procedure; others may be ameliorated by pressure of alert public opinion. In general, I accept Samuel Felton's verdict, that corporations, like individuals, prosper in degree as they serve the public honestly and fairly.

Corporations have been described as "soulless," and from the nature of their legal origin, the description has a certain validity. But, after all, "soul" is impossible of satisfactory definition. There is no room for metaphysical reflection in the corporation; yet, if "soul" be the source of faith, — "the substance of

things hoped for, the evidence of things not seen," —
corporations may be soulful, since through them men
bring visions to reality. Daily some corporation de-
livers, after a long obstacle-race, a message of achievement to its waiting Garcias — the stockholders. And
if "soul" be the motive behind square dealing in the
market-place, the best corporations are at least as
soulful as the best individual traders. Littleness and
trickiness are boon companions. Where policy counts
more than personality, the corporation possesses conscience; its failures to play fair come more often from
heedlessness than from design. Its stake is too great
for meanness, but the corporation has its blind side —
the feelings.

However, the case for the recognition of the corporation as the most practical way out of the present
discord rests upon more solid grounds than mere feeling. Yet with all its faults, the corporation is the most
successful agency of human coöperation yet devised
by the mind of man. In one account the savings and
inheritances of thousands are massed for use; energies
and talents of masses of individuals are sifted and applied intelligently to the making and distributing of
intricate goods over wide areas. Science searches
every phase of business, and genius climbs the ladder
in record time. In an age tending toward socialization,
with a people much preferring even predatory individualism to lifeless state-control, the middle course
lies in the path of group-organization, midway of
which we find the corporation, strongly entrenched in
law and custom. Consequently, being what we are,

where we are, let us use the corporation in the social advance, before abandoning it for the untried, and before settling down in discontented acceptance of things as they are.

Effectively as the corporation brings individuals into coöperation for economic ends, many industrial activities, proceeding under that form, strain the social fabric, and thwart the play of the human spirit. Are these anti-social by-products inevitable? Or may they not be overcome, at least in part, by guiding the evolution of corporations somewhat away from direct and immediate profits, and toward the indirect and deferred profits which come from stability, satisfied labor, and the public esteem? For this man-made and law-born abstraction, the corporation, has been in evolution for more than a century, is considerably different to-day from what it was when the State of New York passed the first general incorporation act in 1811, and will be different again a hundred years hence, no doubt. The question is not, Shall the corporation evolve? but, How shall it evolve? It is somewhat our duty to see that it evolves toward eliminating its social weaknesses instead of toward strengthening its economic excellencies, since competition can be depended upon to continue amply developing the latter.

In viewing this coöperative star of the first magnitude, one notes that the coöperators move on different planes and hold different tenures. The common workman has no authority and no security, for he may be dropped from the pay-roll without notice; whereas

the head of the enterprise has authority over all operatives, and his tenure is usually subject only to returning satisfactory dividends. The chief and his principal
subordinates know that security on the job depends
primarily upon returning service; the workers, on the
contrary, know that they are insecure. They may be
laid off for good reason or none — foreman's prejudice,
cancellation of contracts, onset of business depression.
The most excellent of workers, tragically enough, may
have the ill luck to place himself with an employer
unequal to the strain of competition. This fear of the
future haunts the common man in industry all his
days; combating it is one of the chief motives of his
life, — a motive working out in labor-organizations,
savings accounts, domestic worries, and shop politics,
— good and bad inextricably mixed. The startling
rise in suicide within these twelve difficult months is
another index of the terror that workingmen and
workingwomen face when they lose their jobs. Life
itself is insecure, and insecurity means effort; as the
saying goes, "It puts the fear of God in men's hearts,
and makes them value their jobs." A measure of insecurity is essential to efficiency — I know these
things and do not underrate them. Nevertheless,
there is too much discrepancy now between the relative security of the boss and the positive insecurity of
the worker.

In an inquiry of this sort one treads a narrow trail
between the ethical height and the economic abyss.
Every attempt to scale the height involves a risk of
falling into the abyss, since economic law is as inevi-

table in its operations as gravitation. The bankruptcy chasm is strewn with the wrecks of reputations and institutions once great and too greatly daring. Consequently, he who presumes to chart a course must do so warily, and without assumption of final authority.

As a starting-point let us say that the able and satisfactory employee should hold his job as securely as the boss holds his. That eliminates, at the outset, those of low efficiency in group-operation, whether through inexperience, unsteadiness, or disloyalty to group-interests. Such must ever remain on the margin of employment. But, unfortunately, as things go, depressions recur in which even ably managed corporations must reduce their staffs, in order to remain solvent. So our first adventures toward industrial security should be concerned with these higher human values.

Depressions recur so relentlessly, that statesmen seek relief in state control of credits. Theoretically the state, through the banks, may check expansion in brisk times by withholding credits before the danger-point of expansion is reached, and stimulate employment in dull times by granting credits before the ebb of economic exhaustion has been reached. On the sensible theory that what goes up must come down, it is argued that business can be depressed no further below normal that it has risen above normal; and that, consequently, if the enthusiasm of enterprisers is checked by the state-brake upon credits, the slide into the vale of depression will be checked at a point where business can climb out with slight assistance. Theoretically, and perhaps practically, therefore, the restraining influence of the Federal Reserve Bank is likely to be of social value.

Fairly and intelligently applied, — and we can be entirely sure of neither, — central control of credits should render jobs more secure, by reducing the chances that the efficient boss may be required to lay off his able workmen. But complete security in employment, or any other phase of business, can be bought only at the price of stagnation. Commercial equilibrium is impossible until all the dynamic forces in human society are under control. Trade is born of the instincts, and draws from all their manifestations, big and little. Politicians, diplomats, and generals, all had their fingers in the business pot which boiled over in 1919 and boiled low in 1921. Markets, in the last analysis, are made in child-bed. The instincts that lead our people to produce and consume goods, to plan and dominate, to save and safeguard, defy all attempts at standardization; and as long as Man shall do, can he be kept from occasionally over-doing? Even if we should compass the miracle of dead-level business, as an export nation we should still need to accommodate ourselves to the ups and downs of trade overseas, in localities where our credit writ does not run. Conversely, citizens of a state which binds business too closely through credit-control cannot long hold their own in open markets against traders from more elastic business nations. So, while the state may reduce insecurity, it can bind commercial energies closely only at a price too great for folk of our kind to pay. We must look further before exhausting all the possibilities of harmonizing security in toil with industrial effectiveness.

During the recent depression, certain corporations pursued interesting deviations from normal business practice. Departments, in effect courts, were set up to try cases of dismissal. Instead of accepting the foreman's word on lay-offs, the company delegated authority to qualified persons to judge each case, not only on its economic merits, but also with reference to social significance. A married man was likely to be retained in preference to a single man, and a single man with dependents in preference to an unentangled individual. Plants which might have been run more economically on full time, with fewer helpers, were run on part time with more, to stretch the pay-roll as far as possible. Managements and technical staffs shared wage-cuts in exact proportion to the men, without reference to their higher economic significance. These shifts evidence ethics at work with economics, in the emergency, to divide loss and reduce insecurity. Such innovations have their economic limits, and at best are suited only for particular conditions through short periods.

Two widely advertised cure-alls for unemployment are state insurance and public works. Countries thoroughly industrialized may have no other recourse than state insurance; but even there such programmes involve severe strains. Funds must be built up through taxation in busy years, to cope with the lean years, thus creating a large "frozen credit" applicable in the emergency to buy subsistence — food, fuel, clothing, and shelter — for those out of work and their dependents. These "out-of-works" form merely a part of the whole body of the nation, yet their doles are subtracted by taxation from the earnings of the whole. Moreover, in any depression, the majority of the out-of-works are sure to be the less effective workers and least valuable citizens — the relatively inefficient, irresponsible, and thriftless. Others, of course, will be caught short in the slump; but these down-at-the-heel folk will predominate. Of these, many will loaf on a subsistence basis rather than seek employment. To reduce the individual's incentive to seek employment is a blow at the national economy, because every day that a potential producer is idle means just so much loss to himself, the community, and the state. Emergence from depression requires redistribution of labor-power among plants, industries, and localities, on the basis of most economical use. As long as any person is subsidized to stay where he is, sure of support until his former job is ready, readjustment lags. The state can protect itself against the economic backwash of state insurance only by making its acceptance contingent upon involuntary servitude — the power to force men to work when and where the state dictates. For us, that is impossible. If the country were to continue industrial growth at the old rate, the government might be forced to accept the burden of unemployment insurance without redress; such is the peril of democracy; but as all signs point toward a gradual stabilizing of industry at or below its present limits, the issue may never be forced.

Prosecution of public works, when private work is scarce, presents a fairer face to the analyst. Maximum effectiveness requires, however, careful planning. Plans must be prepared for deferable works, funds accumulated, and skeleton organizations maintained, which may be expanded rapidly by adding unskilled labor as men are thrown out of their regular employments. Wages should be sufficiently below industrial rates to encourage prompt return to industrial employment. Under such conditions morale would be chronically low, and organization unsteady. The public would probably pay as much for the job as it would have paid in brisk times, at high wages. The process is palliative rather than economical, and disappointment easily may follow too great reliance thereon.

Fundamentally, insecurity of work-tenure in industry is no labor problem at all, because the boss is powerless to correct it under present conditions. Since it transcends the employer's power of adjustment, unemployment is rather a social problem, with roots running back to feudalism. In English industrial history, of which our development is an extension, it traces directly to the enclosures of common lands, to which village workers had access for subsistence when cut off from wage-jobs. Insecurity, indeed, is the other side of the shield of freedom; a free man is free either to stand or fall; a bond holds a man up in distress just as it holds him down in prosperity. Every factor, therefore, which has contributed to turn dependence into independence and independence into interdependence, is in part responsible for the insecurity of industrial employment. Thus, a reorientation of industry, in which all those factors participate, is required in order to ameliorate naturally their resultant insecurity.

For individuals to stand alone, economically, becomes more difficult. To be useful, a man must ally himself, directly or indirectly, with others in toil. In large-scale industry this community of interest in producing and marketing of goods engages many thousands in well-defined, legally functioning organizations. Here, obviously, is a rock upon which to build.

At root, the fundamentals of subsistence are food, clothing, shelter, and fuel. Lack of these is what men fear most when their jobs go by the board. They can dispense with comforts and luxuries for a time, without damage and even with benefit; will do so gladly when their enthusiasms are roused, as in war. Given these, a man can hold out; his standard of living may fall uncomfortably, still he and his will live to see better times, no matter how low prices fall.

The farmer has his living; he can survive on his produce; can warm himself with wood; the landlord is not hounding him for rent from month to month: and, if need be, he can wear homespun like Isak of Sellenraa. That explains why, in pinches, the countryside can and does absorb so many marginal workers driven from the mills. The boys from the factory towns, pushed back to the old homestead, find plain fare and ample space — plenty of both, such as they are; and if Nature has endowed them with brains, time to think.

There was a time, in England, when marginal workers had their own land — common land. When wages were lacking, they worked for subsistence. The shift was easy, because the industries were village concerns. Then, new tools were developed, and became concentrated in the towns. Means of industrial production were shifted from villages to towns, common lands enclosed, the marginal worker's refuge upon the land destroyed; and thenceforward, down to the present, insecurity in labor has kept pace with urban development.

Ever since industry took to the towns and set sail toward intense specialization and automatization, its insecurities have impelled revivals of communal production. Idealists like Robert Owen have tried to reëstablish the partnership between industry and agriculture by taking industrial tools back to the land. Mostly these experiments failed: some soon, through inability of the coöperators to agree on division of power and profits; others faded away unmourned, through sheer stagnation. They could not maintain virility in uniformity. If the vital spark of human rivalry won, the commune was destroyed; if uniformity won, the commune decayed, because the spur to adaptability had been cast outside along with the rebels. The root-cause of break-up or decay was chronic inability to pro-rate rewards and responsibilities according to the economic significance of the several producers. If the community were democratic, each shared alike produce and responsibility. None save dullards were completely satisfied; their superiors bickered the project into oblivion. If the community were patriarchal, it became too wooden to meet the dynamic environment set up by its neighbors — free men coöperating in government, toil, and trade.

The weakness of the commune, at bottom, is its inability to measure and reward services. Given a coöperating group possessed of ability and means so to discriminate, there is no reason why such a group could not reunite industry and agriculture on an efficient basis. This the corporation might do. It already rewards many of its workers on the basis of their economic significance through varying work-rates; and the ease with which reward may be apportioned through shares-ownership would permit even adventitious earnings to be distributed with far more regard to the individual contribution to the joint product and individual stake in the enterprise, than the commune possibly could do on its one-man, one-mouth, one-vote basis. Theoretically, a corporation owning land enough to provide its workers with fundamental subsistence could maintain its organization intact at all times; a skeleton organization of experienced farmers could cultivate extensively for profit during brisk times, with details of extra helpers from the mill during harvest; while in depressions the land could be cultivated intensively by more laborers. Farming in its major activities is seasonal, and certain corporations would find it economical to make most of their factory produce in the winter, devoting the summer to agriculture. This seasonal shift, in itself, would be an escape from monotony, a step forward in both mental and physical hygiene, for the workers on automatic machinery.

In accepting the back-to-the-land movement for the corporation as the vital element in regaining a reasonable security for labor, one need not push the idea to absurd lengths. Manifestly such a move would be illogical for many corporations; moreover, in order to relieve the social tension caused by insecurity, it must be remembered that only the marginal workers — at the most twenty per cent — need protection against the "downs" of industry, and then only for limited periods. The efficient employees of efficient employers, even in the darkest days, continue to gain subsistence at their accustomed tasks, since trade never stops entirely. Certain lines of production, moreover, especially those in which raw material is cheap, fabrication simple, product durable, and of relatively stable economic significance, reduce their staffs only slightly in ordinary depressions, because they are safe in stocking up heavily on a low-wage level against the certainty of renewed demand. On the other hand, producers of goods containing a luxury element, which causes rapid fluctuations in the economic significance of those goods in the market, take heavy risks in amassing surpluses. Workers in such industries are relatively insecure. Producers of such goods, however, have much at stake in maintaining their organizations in shape to take quick advantage of market opportunities; hence it is in such lines that industry logically may be expected to leave the city and come to grips on the land with a basic difficulty of modern industry — insecurity for labor.

The corporate form, by making feasible the sharing of rewards according to economic significance, removes one of the barriers separating industry and agriculture. The automatic machine removes another — the skill-barrier. Labor now flows, as we have seen, from country to city, from farm to mill, and back again. While the industrial process, as a whole, has been growing more complex, the contribution of the individual machine-tender to that process has been growing more simple. When tools were simple things, they were close to the soil: now that the tools themselves incorporate the skill-function, their operation is simple enough to make land-labor efficient beside them, and *vice versa*. Their demand upon labor intelligence is no greater, probably less, than that of the simple tools of the pre-industrial era. Hence modern tools can be brought back to the land, under certain conditions and in certain industries, with no considerable loss of economic efficiency, and, in some cases, with definite gains in efficiency. Given just and efficient transportation, fair railway rates, and good roads, many sorts of goods may be produced as cheaply, or even more cheaply, in villages within fifty miles of the swollen town as in the town itself. One sees already the beginnings of industrial migrations from large cities to towns and villages — shifts inspired by economic motives solely. This tendency seems likely to develop slowly, until enough industries have reoriented themselves as regards subsistence to reduce the insecurity of the whole body of labor. These questions, the most fascinating in the entire range of this inquiry, are being elaborated and closely analyzed by my friend and coworker, Ernest F. Lloyd, who was kind enough to place the fruits of his long business experience and later research freely at my disposal.

Corporations, the economic significance of whose product fluctuates widely, are likely to accept this insecurity phase of their labor problem seriously in the future. One can picture a landed industrial corporation taking on its men as potential stockholders, as coöperators. Its selective process would be carefully ordered with reference to mental as well as physical hygiene; an effort to assay the whole man as well as his muscles and senses. The worker would be picked, not so much because he is needed, as because he is wanted. Attention would be paid, not only to his capacity for work, but also to his dependability as a citizen and comrade, his outlook on life, his influence upon, and acceptability to, his fellow workmen and their families, with whom he associates in leisure. His introduction into the shop would be in the nature of an initiation, the binding of one to many, the acceptance of enduring responsibilities, the pledging of one's character to the upholding of a group-character, a connection not lightly to be entered upon, because likely to endure for long.

Such a corporation — in effect a work-clan—would necessarily be interested in how its employees lived and played — in sufficiency and decency of housing, and ordering of community recreation. In short, such a corporation would be, like the commune, a self-sufficient grouping of self-respecting folk; but in certain vital respects it would be unlike any commune known to history. It would possess superior tools, and show a greater variety of incomes and living standards; but more distinguishing would be its division of owner-ship and reward upon the basis of individual, trans-ferable shares. Stockholders, by delegation of author-ity as now, would admit individuals to, or dismiss them from, membership; but the dismissed would continue to own his shares and their accumulations during employment, with full rights of sale. In order, however, to protect the group in such transfers, cer-tain adjustments in corporate law would have to be made.

Since economic development was but one of several factors contributing to the growth of industrial in-security, the ameliorating process must embody other adjustments. Corporations are creatures of the law, and law has limited as well as promoted their develop-ment. Consequently, there are steps toward security which can be accomplished only through legal revi-sions. Present legal barriers to the extension of the coöperative principle inside the corporation must be qualified; and in this release public approval of the newer concept is the logical compelling force.

The present legal concept of the corporation, ar-rived at by applying the shares idea, with strict logic, to private property, vests the reality of the corporation in the holders of its common shares. The public con-cept, on the other hand, more often identifies the cor-poration with its outstanding personality: United States Steel is Judge Gary; Standard Oil persists in being Rockefeller. The workers conceive that reality, however, as located in the front office, from which proceeds power to hire and fire. But the man in the front office may see the reality of the corporation as hanging in the air above scattered directors, who occasionally meet, hear reports, and decide policies. Or, if his directors merely ratify his recommendations, his situation may be such that he knows the corporate court of last resort to be the banker who discounts the corporation's accommodation paper, and floats its securities among his clientele, vouching for the corporation to the financial world and the saving public. The great "Class A" corporations would be impossible without him. But, the banker is a permissive and controlling agent, not a positive, constructive, and operating force, except when he steps upon dangerous ground outside of his fiduciary relation.

All these views, in the intense light of the present, appear a little out-of-date; but perhaps the most antiquated of all is the judicial view. When common stock in great corporations is sold on exchanges as freely as sugar in corner groceries, when lists of common-stock holders vary day by day, and only a fraction of those stockholders profess to know anything about the processes and policies of the corporations, it seems a bit old-fashioned for the law to point to that shifting mob of humans, and say: "There's your corporation, each according to his holding." When common stock represents the company's assets unimpaired by mortgage, there is wisdom in that view; but the fact is that nearly all large corporations have pledged their plants as security on borrowings up to the value of those holdings at forced sale.   What common-stock holders own is usually a slender equity in the property, and a good-will which may easily become no good.   In addition, they have the gamble of future earnings. Expectations as to the amount of those excess earnings set the market-value of common stocks.   To insist that those standing upon this raw edge of adventure, and voting by proxy "sight unseen," are the ones who hold power of purse over the nation's industries and nearly half its people, is simply not true in any broad economic, social, or political sense.

The fact is that the corporation is the corporation. Not in the part, but in the whole, resides its reality. Not alone capital, but also labor, give life and meaning to the enterprise; neither common-stock holders by themselves, nor managers by themselves, are the corporation; but all who have funds invested therein in any form, and likewise all who work for the corporation — all these, coöperating on the bases of innumerable bargains under the law of the land, make up the reality of the corporation.   Their totality is the corporation.   Individuals pass in and out; the institution inherits their good work and bad, gradually acquiring a code and method, a group-personality.   The intangible, impersonal being becomes a living thing, which dies when taken apart.   Yet so important are these business groups to state and people, that the extinction of a great corporation is a calamity.   As in the passing of a feudal barony, many must shift uncomfortably, in perplexity, and oft in woe.

The state, at present, guards the public to some extent against these difficulties in respect to corporations classed as public utilities. These must operate at all hazards; give service even at a loss; the mails must move in time of strike. The public stake in these operations is so heavy, their continuance so vital to civilized life, that the state, to preserve itself, insists that their wheels keep moving. Every year the concept of what constitutes a public utility is broadened. The United States uses the courts and the military to keep coal coming out of the ground, because coal is now a political as well as an economic necessity.

One of the first and most significant steps toward writing into law the fundamental and common interest in continuous corporate functioning was taken in the Canadian Industrial Disputes Investigation Act of 1907. Canadian corporations performing services or delivering goods essential to the public welfare may not lock out their men without investigation by the state, due procedure, delays, and public hearings. Employees of such corporations may not walk out without meeting the same conditions. This establishes the public interest as paramount in certain essentials. The more recent Kansas Industrial Court goes a step further in the same direction, in declaring the production and distribution of food, fuel, and clothing to be invested with a public interest so vital that (in effect) continuity of operation shall apply thereto.

The line between public utilities and other corporations simply will not stay put. Of late, the United

States government and several of its subdivisions
have handled labor crises in coal-mining as if the
mines were public utilities, — which they are, in fact,
— while avoiding establishing them as such in law.
In due time, no doubt, law will follow fact in this respect, as in others. And if a coal-mine shall be kept
open despite the labor and capital directly involved,
why not other enterprises producing goods and services vital to the public? In general, I think, every
corporation employing enough labor and capital to
bring wares or services to market in any considerable
quantity is, and ought to be rated, a public utility. If
this seems too broad a generalization, the way to con-
strict it is to refuse corporate charters to business organizations so minute in size that their operation or
decease presents no difficulty to consumers or the
community. As a matter of fact, corporate charters
are too freely granted by most of the states — a laxity
which results in promotion scandals on the one hand,
and in individuals hiding behind the limited liability
safeguard, on the other. The mere acceptance of the
principle that every corporation is a public utility,
and a means toward group-coöperation and subject to
control as such, would go far toward correcting these
current abuses of corporate provisions.

If the foregoing seems a shocking invasion of the
institution of private property, beware of what is to
follow! I accept the institution of private property as
an obvious result of human instincts and a valuable
motive-force in civilization. I would as soon think of
quarreling with it as with a result of gravitation. Yet

the institution of private property is merely an adjustment between private and public interests, personal and social instincts. Where government ownership promises any pronounced social advantage, let it be applied. But warily, for government is such a feckless manager, that it is idle to push the public-utility theory of the corporation far enough to include all the means of production. However, in order that corporations may work out to the ultimate their potentialities for coöperation, some group-grip upon private capital industrially employed is essential.

At bedrock, successful coöperation in industry depends upon having something to divide. A coöperative enterprise, in which all workers share upon the basis of discoverable economic significance, would be as dependent for discipline and harmony upon the returns from its labors as a corporation in which workers have no share. Brains must be compensated in one way or another, interest paid on invested capital, funds set aside against contingencies. The worker who pays in a hundred dollars wants his per cent as much as or more than the outside investor who risks his thousands. However, the worker has contributed somewhat more than the outsider toward the creation of that dividend. It is difficult to measure exactly the contribution of any individual's brain or brawn, study or labor-pain, to any corporate result, and compensate it exactly on the pay-roll. Few employers make the effort; they buy their labor in the open market, where men are under pressure to sell their time. So it may be said that corporate earnings contain a leakage which labor has lost, and capital has gained, an adventitious profit, not normally by any means as large as extremists claim, but something over and above the rental value of the money used, figured at the "going rate." The quarrel over the division of profits is serious only as it applies to this indefinite element in the industrial equation, since employees generally recognize that capital must secure a reasonable reward, else there is no incentive to save and no capital to hire.

Obviously the workers in any corporate group — I make no distinction between office and shop — should get this leakage, if a sane method of recovering and distributing it can be found, short of upsetting the wage-system. To this end I believe, in common with my friend Lloyd, that corporations henceforth chartered should be vested with the right of eminent domain over their common stock; empowered, that is, to buy such stock from non-employees at its intrinsic worth, whenever this class of security is desired for re-sale to employees and none is available at unforced sale. This would restrain the speculation that irritates labor so acutely, and so often embarrasses conservative managers as well, by divesting industrial capital of its *entrepreneur* function and recognizing it frankly for what it has become — a commodity. This would give the men behind the goods assured opportunity to increase reward through sharing adventitious profit, to the extent that thrift or efficiency gives them control over common stock. Corporate rights to recall stock for coöperative ends might be abused, and safeguards would have to be thrown around any plan; but

on the theory that most men and most corporations
are honest, the apparent advantages recommend a
trial. Once capitalists realize the greater safety of investment in enterprises binding employees closely to
themselves through stock-ownership, the way will be
cleared for setting up a no-par-value common stock,
acquirable in whole, eventually, by the working group
and sharing control with invested capital on terms
mutually agreeable and well defined. Leeway, of course,
should be left by the law, in order that the various
interests involved may bargain themselves into substantial harmony. Freedom to bargain, here as elsewhere, is essential.

In approaching these adjustments, we shall en-
counter, and perhaps lose our way in, a maze of
legalism. Forty-eight sovereign states, with as many
corporation codes and innumerable court decisions
pendent therefrom, furnish a tangle from which all
save lawyers shrink in dismay. Some day we shall
need — perhaps bitterly enough — uniform practice
over the whole country for corporations engaging in
interstate commerce; but when or where or how that
can be brought nearer, I do not prophesy. Still we
shall find a way; "needs must when the Devil drives."

The corporation was attended at birth by a mid-
wife, — the Law, — a fussy creature, but necessary
withal. We shall never get these or any changes in
corporate practice wrought without her aid; but even
so, there is still room for the Greathearts of Industry
to go a long way toward giving their corporations a
grip upon the affections of the people, as now they

grip their needs. Some already have gone far in that direction, against the advices of the elders and suspicions of inferiors. Offering advice to such pioneers is insult; to them these words are but recommendations which, along with news of their own accomplishments, they may pass on to backward brothers. For, until the backward brother comes to realize his social significance and the tremendous power for good or evil of this man-made creature he captains, the corporation will remain under the suspicion of the state and the curse of the mob. Especially may we hope that the evolution of the corporation toward greater coöperation and security for the workers will not be a blind process, but one steadied and hastened by the leaders of industry, each applying courageously in his own way, to his particular problem, the utmost altruism that may be used within the limits of sound economy and valid social concepts.

VII

THE JOB AND SOCIETY

IN "The Bronze Woman" the plutocrat's wife says: "Social unrest! Indeed, if the laboring classes want more rest, why don't they take it?" Escorting a more charming, but equally sheltered, representative of the fortunate class to luncheon, I once met a picket-line of cooks and waiters at their moment of impact with the police.

"What are they fighting for?" asked my companion.

"Their jobs," I replied. "Cooks' and waiters' strike."

"Strange," she observed, "that anyone would fight for the chance to stand over a cookstove."

Later, in a serve-self, I tried to enlighten her; but it was love's labor lost. Indeed, I am sure the job is something of a mystery to most of us — an impenetrable mystery to those who never have known insecurity, and hardly better understood by those who live by and for their jobs every day of their lives.

In a list of the things men fight for, the job ranks well toward the top. Many a man, who must be drafted to fight for his country, rushes to the defense of his job with clenched fists. Tame men, who have to be spurred by oratory and propaganda to throw themselves into great causes, come up bristling like terriers for the job's sake. Men who actually hate their jobs nevertheless fight for those jobs, risking broken heads and jail sentences. No fiercer hatred can be roused in human breast than that which flares in the heart of the common man against his enemy on the job — the "scab." I once heard a union leader give his complete opinion of the scab, and, for searing hate, it outdid war profanity.

A man will leave his job on strike, for reasons which appear absurd to the calm observer, and yet rage like mad at whoever steps into his shoes. In his calm moments he may subscribe to the theory that every man has a right to work; but he never concedes to anyone else the right to work at a job that he considers his, by reason of recent occupancy and willingness to return under certain conditions.

He who depends upon a job vests himself with a proprietary interest therein. Instincts remaining immune to legal distinctions, he speaks of "my job," when he may be tossed out of it within the hour. No ordinary human ever doubts that he is entitled to the means of life; therefore, the wage-employee instinctively assumes proprietorship over that which is essential to his life. In industrial civilization the job is essential to the common man. His defense of his job, his reaction against the invader who comes between him and his job, is as instant as his defense of his life, his home, or his woman. His job, indeed, is the first line of home-defense. Job gone, the home is in sore danger; unless another job can be found before the savings go, the home is ruined. Moreover, unless he can keep the job up to standard, he cannot keep his home or himself up to standard. The job is the measure of social fitness, of his standing in the community; by it the common man rises and by it he falls. Hence the apparent anomaly, of a man fighting for that niche in the workaday world which he walked out of, is no anomaly at all. The striker leaves the job, not of his own free will, but impelled by a conviction that the job needs improving. It is still, in his view, his job; but not worth keeping on existing terms except as a last resort, under pressure of necessity. When he strikes, he expects to return.

Carleton Parker goes the whole way to accepting the job-man's point of view. "The job," he says, "is the worker's property, because the latter has nothing else." That is sophistry: property is based on possession, not lack. And the jobless worker has something else: his time, his arms and legs, muscles, nerves, powers of will and mind, all of which may be taken into the market and sold, as preliminary to the setting up of another job on such terms as the market offers. Property, on the contrary, is tangible, transferable. Two men can trade properties without the consent of a third; they cannot so trade their jobs. The job, in short, is not property, but is, instead, a personal relationship, which, like so many others, is fast becoming a social relationship.

In a time of depression, large numbers of jobs vanish into thin air. Within a week, a thousand jobs may depart from a community because of the market's unwillingness to take the produce of the jobs at the terms offered. The employer must retrench; to delay brings danger of bankruptcy. The men so laid off have n't their jobs, and the employer has n't them, and cannot hope to re-create them until he can induce the market to take his accumulated stocks. He would much prefer to have his plant working full time; each slack day costs him, or his corporation, dearly for depreciation, interest charges, and overhead expense. But for the life of him he cannot revive those jobs until the market, properly courted, comes to his rescue. Until then, all he possesses is the mere shell of the vanished jobs — the work-places, standing-room, and the tools of production upon which the market of consumers enforces temporary idleness.

So the job, having departed from both employer and employee, awaits the commanding touch of the market before it can live again. What, pray, is the market? None other than society, the totality of persons and institutions in the trading area. The job depends, therefore, upon consumption; if jobs belong to anyone, they belong to society. Which is equivalent to repeating, in another way, that jobs are not property, because society owns nothing. Individuals and their various associations of record own everything appropriable that is worth appropriating. The state, our most inclusive association of record, is held loosely accountable by society for order and general well-being; but until the state can force folk to live according to regimen, consuming thus and so and not otherwise, the job remains at loose ends, in the air. The free job — free in the sense that it exists as a result of bargaining among free men under the law — is a result of freedom in the larger sphere. It was not present in serfdom, but came into being with freedom; and all efforts to harness it involve a diminution of freedom.

The unions, when they try that, encroach upon the liberties of both employers and union members; the employers, when they try it, trespass upon the liberties of individuals; and the state that tries it edges away from liberty. To stabilize the social order, progress in that direction may be necessary; nevertheless, it is an infringement of personal liberty, and every prospective advance in that direction ought to be judged from that point of view — as an invasion of freedom.

The right to work means one thing to John Doe, and something else to his neighbor. Capital and labor — each has its interpretation; the spokesmen of both often talk nonsense; there are rogues and dullards on both sides of the fence. But certain aspects of the case are clear as day. No rights can long remain vested where the corresponding duties are refused. If labor insists on the right to quit, it cannot logically insist on the right to work. Labor, it seems to me, should cleave to the right to strike, because the exercise of that right has brought the masses real boons; but, if so, it must cease claiming that work for pay, on the materials and with the tools of others, is a right. Work on such terms is not a right, but a social privilege. Some day it may become a right: there are tendencies working in that direction now; but the process can be completed only by men voiding other rights they now hold dear, and assuming as duties inhibitions they now hold to be intolerable.

Both strike and lockout are weapons inevitably called into play when employer and employee contest to determine the conditions of jobs after bargaining fails. Use of one cannot be denied fairly, unless the other is also denied; neither, in my opinion, can be dispensed with while men remain free alike to work and own. However, let it be noted that neither strike nor lockout is used until bargaining has been invoked, and has failed, either because one side would not bargain, or because the bargain, once begun, was not completed.

Moreover, neither strike nor lockout is applied unless the applier is convinced that he can win by so doing. No body of men ever yet went on strike for pure principle, in a cause they knew to be hopeless; and no employer ever locked out men simply to make good a point in policy. This is a rough world, but as yet its inhabitants fight for objectives instead of excitement. The railway unions stayed at work in November, 1921, simply because a majority of their leaders became convinced that a strike at the date advertised would be lost. Their eleventh-hour decision not to strike was merely good generalship, with nothing of altruism or accommodation to public needs in it. But better generalship would have been (1) to lie low, like Br'er Rabbit, for a better opportunity; or (2) to say, "We yield to save the public inconvenience," which would have been as untrue as most propaganda, but time-serving and face-saving — a proclamation for political purposes only.

Evolution toward industrial security involves inevitably some diminution of industrial freedom for individuals; each generation must choose between having more of the one and less of the other; both cannot be maintained coincidently. The drift now is toward security and away from freedom; the social order gains at the expense of individualism; but thus far the fringe of freedom sheared off has been of small value, because reality departed from it before the knife began to cut. When individuals find it increasingly difficult to produce independently of others; when many are under practical necessity to toil on materials and at machines owned by a corporation which, in turn, is owned by numbers of scattered stockholders, there is no paramount advantage in retaining, undisturbed, arrangements effective when individualism in toil was real and personal independence easily maintained.

To put the case concretely, the laborer who could escape from the pay-roll to free land was in a far different situation from his successor, who finds the national domain practically appropriated and farm-lands selling above the capitalized value of their earnings. The freedom of the first producer was absolute: he could go or stay; the other's is relative: he can go only under favoring circumstances not easy to control. The first might resent an interference which the other would welcome, providing it brings compensation in the matter of security. And, likewise, an employer who is keen to defend his right to exploit an expanding market as he sees fit, may welcome restraint when he sees trade slowing down, and realizes that the untrammeled instincts of enterprisers inevitably lead to over-production, which threatens his own security, along with that of his employees. Federal control of credits, which, in the last analysis, means control of business and a more stabilized production, was not badly received by the business world.

The fringe of industrial freedom is now dead tissue, though once tingling with life. The causes of decay in that tissue are many; but prominent among them must be listed the growing influence of automatism, standardization, and interchangeability in fabricating goods. Machinery has increased the insecurity of the common man's position in the wage-system, by increasing the number of potential competitors for his job. The balance between security and individualism has been destroyed, with the result that personal freedom in work-relations no longer seems worth fighting for, and a new balance must be struck. When personal skill was a prime factor in industry, the individual artisan occupied a fairly safe position, because substitutes were few — a security which had its inevitable offset in the fact that, since shop-practices were not standardized, he had difficulty fitting in elsewhere, and so was more or less tied to the job. The point is that, if he was tied to the job. so likewise was the job tied to him. The management disliked to see him get out of town.

Note the contrast with the present. To-day, he who does ordinary work in a plant highly automatized is in potential competition with every idle man in a far-spread labor market—and, unless the task is arduous indeed, with many women, also. The skill-barrier has been trampled down so completely by the

Iron Man, that whoever possesses ordinary intelligence and strength can take the machine-tender's place after short instruction. The common man's grip on his job has loosened. If he does n't like the place, let him get out; plenty of persons can fill his shoes in short order. And if he must be laid off, there is no need to worry about keeping a string on him until happier times. Out with him; and never mind what becomes of him. Let the man, the community, and the state fret over that.

I do not mean to say that all employers, or any considerable proportion of them, are so ruthless; some of them have gone so far as to risk insolvency out of human, non-economic consideration for their help; but that is the power which automatic machinery puts into employers' hands — power which the least ethical will be prompt to use; power which competition may force even the most ethical to use, in order to keep his corporation solvent.

The increasing influence of automatic machinery promotes industrial insecurity in another way, — by speeding up market gluts, — as a result of which jobs vanish as if by magic and are only gradually reëstablished. The first English factory equipped for interchangeable manufacture — that at Portsmouth, in 1808 — at once multiplied the productivity of the individual producer of ships' blocks by ten. From that time on, we have gone along multiplying man-power as measured in goods, and there is apparently no limit at which the process, economically, can be stayed. In spite of tremendous efforts to educate backward peoples in wants, and force goods into use in trading areas not accustomed to them,—efforts which created part of the background of the World War, — market gluts and their resultant depressions are recurrent phenomena.

I know that plenty means cheapness and extended use; nevertheless, it is apparent that the social, political, and financial fabric of civilization is not sufficiently sensitive to accommodate itself to these increases in production rapidly enough to avoid vast and poignant distress. Recurrently, production runs ahead of consumption; population increases, but not swiftly enough; wants increase, but not fast enough; the standard of living rises, but not far enough. The patient, society, unable to digest such enormous masses of goods, becomes nauseated and needs purging. Doctors rally to the bedside; nevertheless, recovery is slow. All sorts of persons suffer in these fits of social sickness, but those who suffer most are they who customarily labor for wages with the tools of others. Given the ballot, it is inevitable that they should use it to combat such difficulties.

From the standpoint of national economy, a capable and willing man out of a day's work is a calamity. Multiplied by millions, the situation is a threat against the state. There was a time when England said to her unemployed: "Emigrate"; then she kept them up out of the rates; now she combines state relief and doles. No one dares to hint that starvation is expected of the unemployed. Some reactionaries may think it, but they dare not say it. In such a pass the government, torn between threats of insolvency and revolution, must find jobs — a task for which the state is by its nature unfitted, and which America, more favorably situated, may avoid. Not that we would behave differently under like extremity; but, by taking thought, we may escape the extremity, at least until our population becomes considerably more dense than it is to-day.

Fortunately, the automatic machine and public education provide an ameliorating influence. As wages tend toward a common level, and capital gradually loses its *entrepreneur* function, considerable progress will be made toward a relative equalizing of incomes. There would remain, of course, incomes derivable from rent and interest; but for all that we can see to the contrary, super-taxes will discourage such accumulations and gradually shred away large wealth-holdings. As wages are leveled, not absolutely but relatively, so also are incomes likely to be leveled relatively. This involves, of course, a reduction in society's power to produce capital by saving — a serious sacrifice, no doubt (but one which apparently must be made, in order to permit the producer to consume more nearly the equivalent of his product). If production and consumption were exactly equal there could be neither glut nor dearth; but, even in a static world, capital would be destroyed in use, and must be restored, in order to keep labor effective.

This hazily forecasted change involves time, perhaps more than the passions of the post-war era will permit. Meanwhile the virtues of both strike and lockout will continue to be abused, and government will continue to burn its clumsy fingers in the fires of class-discord. I detest programmes, and would avoid even the appearance of prescribing definite remedies. But if you insist on a programme, — and the ordinary person will not be content without some positive direction, — then, without any fear of the consequences, I recommend the coöperation of working shareholders in corporations animated by zeal for the group good, but adhering to the sound practice of rewarding workers according to their economic significance in production and their thrift in contributing capital to the enterprise. Where feasible and advantageous, such groups should ensure their continuity by possessing a grip on the land — now, as ever, the source of man's subsistence and his haven of refuge in all ages. Some, at least, of the millions who now live in fear for their jobs from one day to another could thus anticipate the day when the further organization of life and industry, by methods impossible to foresee, will combine reasonable security for rank-and-file producers with all the freedom compatible with such tenure.

The job is a social grant, as well as a lease on life; and, unless all signs fail, it must eventually gain social guaranties. But whatsoever those guaranties are, they must be bought and paid for at a price. Our bitter quarrel over the job is founded on a false assumption of proprietorship over a relationship which eludes appropriation. Soon or late those vitally concerned are going to realize that truth, cease fighting, and begin to negotiate more constructively.

VIII

WAR AND WORK

IN America we invent, manufacture, and use in the production of goods, an infinite number of machines; but we pay scant heed to the effect of these machines upon the evolution of society. Out here, in our great Middle West machine-shops, where the automatic principle of machine production has reached its highest development and broadest application, we possess tools superior to those of Paris. Yet it would never have occurred to any of us to say in 1914, as did Bergson in addressing the French Academy: —

"Many years hence, when the reaction of the past shall have left only the grand outlines in view, this perhaps is how a philosopher will speak of our age. He will say that the idea, peculiar to the nineteenth century, of employing science in the satisfaction of our material wants had given a wholly unforeseen extension to the mechanical arts, and equipped man, in less than fifty years, with more tools than he had made during the thousands of years he had lived upon earth. Each new machine being for man a new organ, — an artificial organ, — his body became suddenly and prodigiously increased in size, without his soul being, at the same time, able to dilate to the dimensions of his new body."

Bergson pictures the "machinate mammal" of Butler's striking phrase as a dread, autogenetic being, adding limbs and organs *ad infinitum*, without corresponding growth of soul —a modern monster set going by our busy Frankensteins, the inventors. Let us consider, rather, man in society, organized into states, and observe some of the political and social results which have followed, and are likely to follow, multiplication of man-power by machinery.

Multiplying man-power by machinery sets in motion certain forces and tendencies in key with — but not at all points parallel to — those set in motion in other times by brisk breeding. However generated, new peaks of human energy strain social and political systems evolved to carry currents less high. Unless the current is cut down, or the system of distribution readjusted to carry the new peak-load, something breaks. War is simply one method of restoring equilibrium between the kinetics of human energy and the statics of social order.

Machine use, on the expanding scale of recent years, multiplies goods production over and above any point attainable by natural increase without machine assistance. Power over machines enabled the coal-and-iron members of the great-nations group to establish world-leadership in the years between the industrial revolution and the World War. Not only did population in the industrial states increase absolutely, but the effectiveness of those increased populations in wealth production multiplied over and over. States with more machines assumed preponderant political influence over those with less.

Because the nations of leading power at the opening of the twentieth century were all white and all Christian, a false idea arose that this overlordship rested upon race or religion; but Japan's entrance, following victory over Russia, proved the acid test of world-power to be industrial prowess. Enough productivity to furnish, year after year, a considerable excess of goods for export, and to support naval and military forces proportionate to the resulting extensive overseas interests — these were the prime desiderata of power; and the nation possessing them could be sure of its place in the sun, regardless of color or the constitution of its godhead.

Machine-power not only strengthened nationalism by slowing down dispersion through emigration, but also intensified it, by generating real need for group action to ensure subsistence from foreign sources. To make the industrial centre secure, its economic hinterland must be likewise secure; states were constantly urged by groups oppressed by the conviction of insecurity to move outward toward the control of that ever-widening hinterland, without whose produce and consumption the industrial complex at home must languish in unprofitable depression.

In earlier times natural increase set in motion centrifugal forces, which machine increase shifted into centripetal forces. Nations in effective possession of coal and iron held their nationals, because machines permitted the use at home of more labor and more capital per acre. Instead of sending forth surplus population at the former rate, the industrial states sent forth, in ever-increasing volume, surplus goods to compete with those of their rival nationals in world-markets. The descendants of men who had won sustenance at the spear-point in forced migrations now fought one another with goods, and recorded their victories in ledgers instead of sagas. Upon the profitable and certain sale of these goods depended national solvency and domestic content, the hunger or plenty of millions of wage-earners, the revenues which supported governments, military establishments, educational institutions — in short, modern Western civilization. Realizing the vulnerability of their economic supports, the industrial societies of the Old World grew more and more state-conscious, and drifted into more and more echinate relations one with another. Thus modern nationalism developed a sinister accent.

Given the determining mechanisms, this development was sure as fate. Arteries of national existence, inextricably interwoven, came to thread the Seven Seas. Though the bulk of imported nourishment grew in stabilized quarters, certain essentials of industrial life were gathered from lightly settled districts of uncertain political complexion, where the white man's code did not run. Concessions and capitulations, extra-territoriality and economic penetration — these satisfied neither natives nor invaders. Willy-nilly, the situation made for imperialism. Wherever moneys were owing and courts were not; wherever raw materials needed in the mills back home could be produced; wherever goods could be sold to the heathen if the latter could be educated sufficiently in wants; wherever capital could be multiplied by exploiting cheap labor — there industrial societies, though located on the other side of the earth, had stakes, vital stakes of existence. The temptation was powerful, indeed, to change these stakes of existence into stakes of empire. Africa was partitioned; western Asia became a bickering ground; China was divided into spheres of influence, and must soon have been parceled out if the United States, not yet hard pressed economically, had not initiated the saving reprieve of the "Open Door."

So far toward the war had the nations traveled by the beginning of the century. Thereafter came intrigue after intrigue for adjustment and review. Only by stating and restating the Monroe Doctrine, in terms which would have amazed Monroe, were we able to fend off itching hands from South America, perchance to keep for ourselves freedom of action in that quarter at some later date. Elsewhere the game went on with ever-increasing openness as the economic needs of Europe became more acute. The nations looked sharply to navies, coaling-stations, merchant marines, as so much national insurance under the conditions imposed by the Iron Man. Popular hate must be roused, to wring funds for naval expansion from parliaments and taxpayers. Enter propaganda, the press doing its share, and navy leagues the rest. Diplomatic incident followed incident, well named because so obviously incidental eruptions of the primary force that made peace ever more difficult to keep. Algeciras, London, The Hague — all vain while factory-wheels continued to move at an ever-accelerated pace, and statesmen continued thinking in terms of politics instead of economics. Back of all this diplomatic jockeying and military picketing, commercial zeal and naval expansion, — the motor-force behind all these expressions of national will, — operated unceasingly the overload of human energy released by machine multiplication of man-power.

Responsibility for this dangerous evolution rests upon political rigidity rather than upon industrial progress. Internally each of the industrial states maintained such a division of the returns of industry that its full production could not be consumed at home; internationally trade and finance reached planetary proportions without correspondingly broad political and legal controls. Failing such controls, the situation marched swiftly to its conclusion. Almost to the last, either of two denouements was possible — either the boundaries of industrial states must burst under inequalities of pressure generated by increased populations and increased machines, or the machines themselves must be slowed down by eliminating profits from their operation. The first meant war — the World War; the second meant war also, but of a different sort — the war between classes, the social revolution.

In midsummer of 1914, it was nip and tuck which method of bleeding the too-vital patient would be adopted. Had Juarès lived, who knows how changed the face of history might be? The state-war method won the desperate race against time. At the moment, decision rested with certain Germans, who may have been influenced, consciously or unconsciously, by the hovering spectre of social and political revolution.

If deferred then, the decision a little later might have rested upon other persons elsewhere; and if so, the answer must have been the same — war. Useless to apply ethical rules at such a pass; indicting forces is even more absurd than indicting nations. The important thing to understand, here and now, is that, given nationalism as the dominant social fact of the planet, sea-striding industrialism as its dominant economic fact, and the control of weak peoples by strong as its dominant political fact, peace in or near the year 1914 could not be maintained without qualifying one or all of the three. It was not done. There was none big enough to do it. To that extent, the war may be considered inevitable.

Has Europe's blood-letting, *plus* its post-war Socialism and Communism, rid the world of wars bred in the market-place? The situation does not make for confidence. State competition, intensified by hunger, hate, and debt, is not yet restrainable by international bonds. Russia's experiment does not recommend the class-war as a means to peace. Just as industry and nationalism conceived and brought forth the World War, without knowing quite either when or how conception occurred, so they may add to the Martian family in the future. Indeed, certain tendencies of modern industrialism, in its new automatic phase, as yet but dimly understood, seem destined to put even more strain upon the political framework of the planet than that under which the same framework cracked in 1914.

One such aspect of industrialism is its tendency to

spread. Born in England, the factory system has mi-
grated to northwestern Europe, northern Italy, the
United States, and Japan. It has healthy roots in
Canada, less healthy ones in Mexico. It appeared in
Russia, and contributed to that debacle. China is
getting under industrial way, slowly, but with a
steady ponderosity which Ross, Stoddard, and Weale
agree means nothing less than an economic upheaval
certain to affect every nation and individual on earth
as time runs on. India, too, is on the way, quickening
step during the war. Australia, by erecting a tariff
wall, encourages domestic industries. Thus industry
travels; how far can it go?

The spread of industry among colored and Slavic
populations has been retarded appreciably by the fact
that, in the past, industrial production required the
application of certain traits, natural or acquired,
which, for historic reasons beyond the scope of this
paper, are more apparent in the white peoples than
in others. The skill element was paramount. Now,
industry has machines so highly perfected that highly
specialized skill is not required. Ordinary intelligence
and average manual dexterity are the top requirements, from the standpoint of production only, for the
operative or attendant of automatic machines. He
who brings maximum endurance to the shop at minimum cost will profit his employer most. On this basis
the Chinese coolie, at first glance, appears unbeatable.
If not the best individual, his cheapness still may give
his produce an advantage in the market. The Jap-
anese have demonstrated a considerable degree of

Oriental adaptability to modern machines. The Hindu, on test, may not be far behind. And since the tendency in machine-development is always toward less and less mental demand upon the operative, there is the possibility that even more backward peoples than these may some day find machines attuned to their mental and manual capacities. The huge profits likely to follow promptly upon the putting of cheap, low-standard labor at work upon automatic and semi-automatic machines should be enough to ensure that, soon or late, all peoples will be brought to the ordeal by the Iron Man.

But whether browns, blacks, and yellows can withstand this ordeal is another matter. Theoretically, expansion of industry should proceed until export trade in manufactured goods is much curtailed. But there are offsets to consider — capital, coal, iron, oil, water-power. Dearth of these bars industry from many quarters. Far more important, however, are the varying abilities of races and peoples to meet the social and political problems presented by machine industry. The white race is progressive; the historic concept which has motivated Western history gives it a superior elasticity of adaptation to changing conditions. Yet the war proves that even we favored whites could not escape at least one terrific setback resulting from industrial impact. The depth and breadth of present social unrest further emphasizes the difficulties of adjustment on that side of the equation. Since the colored races have not yet been tried in the fiery crucible of industry, no one can prophesy their reaction to the impact of modern industry.

Consider from this angle some of the vital demands that industry makes upon government and upon society. Industry requires a government at once strong and flexible. Government must preserve domestic order against class jealousies that fatten upon the disparity of wealth inevitably arising from industrialism under private ownership — as King demonstrates in his comparison of incomes in Prussia and Wisconsin. It must uphold contracts under conditions in which contractual relations become increasingly complex. It must protect the people from their employers and from themselves; it must maintain such hours of labor and working conditions as will save the workers from being ground down in ruthless competition, or enfeebled by their own weaknesses. It must encourage the public, and find ways and means to compensate it for the social sacrifices involved in industrial production, which compensations must be provided outside of factory walls and enjoyed at leisure. To provide these sedatives requires the presence of an imaginative, strongly functioning public spirit outside of the industrial group, and the finding of funds to make expensive dreams of social progress come true, at least sufficiently to allay discontent.

The dilemma presented by heavy social needs, and the very real danger of overtaxing industry, is not an easy one to solve, even for states highly organized; it may well prove insoluble for states which, like China and Turkey, reveal chronic inability to establish sound public finance. Finally, history gives no ground for believing that industry and autocracy are compatible; in the long run, so strong are the social pressures involved, a successful government of an industrial state must grow out of the conscious will of its people, represent their ideals, and be amenable to those ideals as they change from generation to generation. Even in Japan the advent of industry brought constitutional forms, not yet nationally digested. Those states in which representative democracy had reached its highest expression emerged from the desperate test of war, and the grind of war-production, with the least political and social damage.

Industry prospers best under capitalism and under representative democracy; I cannot conceive industry functioning well under other dispensations. German autocrats might introduce state socialism as they pleased: the fact of autocracy remained a threat to German industry. And because no colored race equals the white in its power to create the social and political setting in which machine industry thrives, I am unable to follow Lothrop Stoddard to the lengths he goes in forecasting the shrinking of the white man's markets in his book, "The Rising Tide of Color."

Indeed, the impact of industry upon colored races seems as likely to weaken them as the reverse. Modern industrialism places both the individual and society under severe and continued strains, physical, mental, moral. The more static the society, the more custom-tied the individual, the more severe the strain. The English people have been evolving with and in industry, under representative government, for six centuries; for two centuries they have been applying power to machines and building up a factory system. All this time they have been building up definite immunities against industrial ills, and definite predispositions to bargain themselves out of industrial ills. Yet they are never out of hot water, politically and industrially. I do not see how peoples without that background, or something like it, lacking alike political flexibility and industrial experience, can stand the attrition of industrial life. Industrialism in its functioning and growth — and it is still growing — requires never-ending readjustments, compromises, and concessions which are born of freedom and responsibility — the right of individuals and groups to bargain freely, and the duty, freely accepted, of living up to the bargain after it is made. Where these concepts have no place in the popular mind, there industry will have rough sledding, and can become efficient only through a system of force and repression which eventually defeats itself.

It is easy, under the automatic régime, for a man to stand beside a machine and produce goods, and difficult for him to stay there and remain a reasonably satisfied, contributing member of a political and social group, strong enough to maintain itself, yet flexible enough to give him reason to believe industrialism worth while. Mexico's experience is a case in point. Diaz, proceeding toward the industrialization of his country with the aid of foreign capital, enterprisers, and engineers, unmistakably bettered the economic condition of Mexican labor. Nevertheless, the peons' ideal of life remained agricultural; Madero won their backing with his promise of forty acres and a mule. Carranza, inheriting from Madero, frankly declared his country's antipathy to industrialism. Whatever his faults, Carranza sized his Indian up correctly. Though the Mexican peon has certain innate capacities for factory work, notably high manual dexterity and stolid patience, he prefers to half-starve on the land rather than work upon modern machines indoors, at wages that would enable him to maintain a higher standard of living. Necessity may bring him to the factory, if we whites insist; but he will remain a rebel, active or potential, against industrial organization so imposed.

The Mexican's instinctive reaction against industrial organization differs in degree, but not in kind, from that of many of our own shop-workers. There develops among the workers in highly automatized plants a chronic dissatisfaction, which cannot be explained away without reference to nerves. It seems to be proof against high wages and good conditions. Welfare-work, bonuses, shop-councils, even profit-sharing do not drive it out. So pervasive is this malady that it might be described as a work-neurosis. Clatter and haste are contributing factors; so also are indoor confinement, monotony of task, distance from the real boss, repression of personality, strict regimentation of effort, and the scant opportunity afforded for the play of the craftsman instinct, the joy in production.

But the basic cause lies deeper. All of us are descended from ancestors who, a comparatively short

time ago, were farmers, hunters, and fishermen with
occasional experience as fighting men. Their work
held considerable variety, called for great outbursts
of physical energy interspersed with frequent let-
downs. They had their labor-thrills along with their
labor-pains. Even the simple annals of the mediæval
poor must have been crowded with adventure, as
compared with the systematic, colorless, bare-of-
drama tasks of the modern factory. Your worker is
there in the factory, not because he wants to be, but
because he needs the money, and can discover no other
means of getting it. Yet there is that stirring within
him which informs him, even before the voice of the
agitator reinforces the conviction, that this is no life
for a real man. He gets, literally, no fun out of his
labors. His environment irks him, and out of that attrition is born an *Arbeitschmerz* as real as the *Welt-
schmerz* that Goethe discovered. Our tenders of machines are being starved in their souls; and while there
may be sedatives for that malady, there is no specific.

That seems to me the root of social unrest in America; and it is probably equally true in Europe. Under
our political and social controls, in a people naturally
robust and hopeful in spirit, the sickness may not run
its course. Though half our mechanics talk radicalism
they vote with the others for Harding, play baseball
in our parks, and get some relief and encouragement
out of being literate citizens of a republic whose evolution tends, however slowly, toward the interests of
the masses.

But what will this chronic work-pain drive other

breeds to do — breeds that get no relief out of sport and voting? Well, to cite the shining example, it seems to have poisoned Russia's industrial workers against the only system of industry under which industry functions profitably in our day; the Communists of Russia come from her few industrial towns. Signs of similar explosions are not lacking in Japan. No matter how shops are organized, no matter how profits are divided, this fraying of nerves in industry continues. Industry may stir temporarily the simple folk of Mandalay and Peshawar; but can they stand the shock any better than the Amerind withstood the white man's methods and the white man's whiskey? Modern industry is strong drink; those who have lived long with it, despite partial immunity born of experience, are none too happy; and those less experienced dally with it at the risk of their health, customs, general effectiveness, and political stability.

Viewing from these angles the possibility of spreading industrialism, a tremendous dilemma presents itself. On the one hand, the economic forces that spread industrialism outward from its English inception are still operative, and more vigorous than before. To the constant of self-interest is added a heightened state-interest flowing from huge debts. These converging interests now have tools at their disposal which admit to efficient production breeds of cheap men not hitherto available as industrial workers. These dynamic forces are not to be denied their trial of strength. On the other hand, peoples about to be introduced to industrialism must overcome grave social and political inhibitions before they cut down materially the demand for the white man's goods, and so restrict his influence in the world. These contrary forces — one set positive, the other negative; one the essence of progress, the other the essence of conservatism — are bound to do battle with one another on the world-stage. Upon the outcome depends the future of terrestrial society.

Alarm as to the outcome has been sounded vociferously enough; and though the warnings may be more strident than the dangers are imminent, still the outlook calls for the highest statesmanship. The trial period, while the old and new do battle in Asia, is sure to be an era of extreme nervousness in international relations. During this period the white nations must strive toward a genuine solidarity, at the very time when their traders and governments are forced by powerful economic motives to cut into each other's markets. At a time, too, when rankling hate persists, and statecraft is still under the shadow of chauvinism. Any statesman who does not make an effort to overcome these difficulties deserves ill of posterity; because the situation is one in which peace must be labored for, and of which war is the logical outcome.

There can be no durable peace, and no effective white solidarity, so long as the coal-and-iron states continue treading the path of economic competition toward another Armageddon. A sword is suspended over civilization, and that sword can be sheathed only by such a reorientation of industrialism as will permit the aggressive nationalism it fosters to die of inanition.

Much may be done by international agreement, with force back of the agreement; more may be done by the forward spirits in each industrial society forcing into public attention these internal adjustments necessary to bring social and political evolution into line with industrial evolution. The more energy goes into internal developments, the less will press outward to complicate international relations. There is plenty of work for all governments to do at home, before their populations recover their pre-war trust in governments.

Every alert man or woman recognizes that the masses are critical of governments in this year of grace. The conviction is growing that the war was of economic origin. Men are no longer willing to turn out war as a by-product of goods — on machines. Since a prime source of belligerency is goods-competition, sovereignty has become a matter of control over machines as well as over men. That is the direction in which competent governments must move; and those which fail to keep step will possess no valid reason for existence in the automatic-machine age. The peoples of the earth look to governments to set up a moral control over machine use; and this instinctive turning to the state for relief is sound to the core, since states are the only groupings of humanity strong enough to harness the Iron Man to the chariot of human well-being.

IX

THE IRON MAN'S LEGACY

WHY all this bother about industry? Why worry ourselves attempting to understand life and evaluate its processes, when our test of life is short and our recommendations of doubtful validity?

The answer is bound to be mixed. For instance, I write this partly to prove my uniqueness among men, since no other could, or would, do this task in just this way. Also, I do it to satisfy my will to power, since to influence other minds is to dominate them in some degree, even though the method be the gentle one of persuasion. But to some extent I do it out of a sense of responsibility to posterity, to the race.

One's feeling of responsibility for the future measures one's progress in civilization. The primal savage bears no such burden; but let him grow ever so little civilized, — to the point, let us say, of founding a home, — and the future overtakes him. He may concern himself only with the possible weal or woe of his own household after he is gone, and the disposition of his trophies and gear; but responsibility for the future is likely to widen and deepen as the social group expands. The clansman gives thought to the future of his clan, the tribesman to the future of his tribe, the citizen to that of his state; and those whose intellects and sympathies transcend state boundaries are fated to feel a responsibility for the future of all men.

Our whole civilization is geared, in one way or another, to the future. There is a selfish motive in that, to be sure, since we expect posterity to pay our public debts. But fundamentally our sense of responsibility for the future is unselfish. We work and save and plan and fret so prodigiously in the present, in the hope that our children and our neighbors' children, unto the thousandth generation, shall live more gloriously than ourselves, and realize more nearly the utmost material and spiritual values of life. Vain thought, perhaps; nevertheless compelling enough to influence not only most public expenditures, but much private spending and giving. Children, born and unborn, are the finite reason for civilization; adults toil to maintain and improve civilization, in order to bestow it as a going concern upon posterity. We fling the torch, and trust that those who catch it may not get their fingers burned as badly as we have.

The thought of Chinese worshiping their ancestors amuses us, yet we proceed with no better reason to worship posterity. The Chinese, at least, know what their ancestors have done to deserve sacrifices, while we have n't the faintest idea whether our descendants are going to be worthy of our sacrifices. We take posterity on faith. Yet, if this element of futurity were eliminated, civilization would be meaningless, a travail not worth while for the masses, and a meaningless adventure in control for the directing class. If evolution is simply change, and not progress; if the human family cannot advance in morality, justice, and fair play beyond existing norms, then all who can might as well go on vacation and let things slump. It is precisely because our sort of man cherishes the idea of race-betterment, that he keeps on trying. He is often betrayed, and more often betrays himself; and when he succeeds he frequently finds the results of change worse than no change would have been; nevertheless the ideal remains undamaged. This habit of looking forward instead of backward, of prospection instead of introspection or retrospection, is what, at bottom, has put the white race in command of human affairs.

Consequently the effect of the functional revolution of the automatic machine upon the race is bound to be the most important of all its effects. Its material advantages are of no surpassing moment, unless they can be transmitted beneficially; its ills are of no great consequence, if they can be overcome before they break down the fibre of the race too far for recovery. In assaying the value of adjustments in industry, whether they be economic, psychological, social, or political, — or a medley of these, — we are bound to consider what their effect is likely to be upon race-evolution. We shall not be here when the verdict comes in; nevertheless there is that in us which insists that we pose the question, make the inquiry, and proceed with the ultimate in view of benefiting posterity.

In spite of the scientists, there is none too much light at hand. The natural laws affecting heredity are still far from precisely outlined; there are gaps in the testimony, which still make life a mysterious, august riddle. Nevertheless, in all humility, let us proceed.

As far as we are aware, every mental and physical attribute of man once possessed definite survival value, and, for all that we know to the contrary, may still possess that value. In a changing environment, over immeasurable periods of time, these became fixed in the main, but continue variable in minors. The average cephalic index of a tribe is approximately standard over the tribe; but few out of many will have heads matching exactly the average measurement for the whole group. The human hand has become standardized at five fingers; yet skin remains unstandardized, and no two humans have the same finger-prints. As the conditions of life change, certain attributes, mental and physical, gain, while others lose, importance. A keen sense of smell is a nuisance to a modern; hence noses grow less sensitive. So, likewise, the subconscious mind is an inchoate network of inherited memories, which it is conceivable we might do without; at times they are most embarrassing; still, for all we know, shifting circumstances may call some of them definitely into consciousness at any moment; and what to a utilitarian seems like useless lumber in the forgotten attic of the mind may prove to be quite the most valuable heritage we can leave our children.

How far the individual mind may be dulled by close daily association with automatic machinery depends, of course, upon the variety of interests that intrigue that mind after working hours, and what defenses it can set up against the inroads of pathological fatigue while at work. To apprehend the factors entering into that phase of the Iron Man's progress, however, is child's play compared with discovering to what extent the effects of such dulling are transmitted to succeeding generations. After interminable argument, we are still far from unanimous upon the relative weight of environment and heredity in determining mind, body, and character. In general, we know that like tends to bring forth like, in certain ratios established by Mendel and dignified by the name of the Mendelian Law; but that there are limits to this sort of determinism may be deduced from De Vries's experiments with "sports." And finally, no one can estimate with any certainty how many generations of minds may be dulled, and how many generations of bodies stunted, before such shortcomings become fixed enough for inevitable transmission. Anywhere within a thousand years, at least, we must qualify the potency of heredity by saying that in a single generation of favorable environment one individual in a race series may advance as far as many generations of his forbears declined; and that the sustaining of favorable environment through several generations may wipe out, for practical purposes, traces of a much longer decline. Nevertheless, we have no reason to bank upon such good fortune coming adventitiously, or by sport, to any racial line; and hence the dependable way to promote race-betterment is by grappling here and now with the degenerating tendencies in our common environment.

The effect of industry upon race is a question so broad that it may be divided into two parts: how far does industry cause average folk to degenerate, and how far does it assist or restrain defectives from multiplying?

Indirect as well as direct effects may be noted in any industrial city. Long habituation to a monotonous, machine-paced task must tend to render the operative less adaptable and less alert than he would be if employed in an occupation permitting more variety of effort and thought. In turn, lessened adaptability renders him less able to cope with his environment successfully. This is a direct effect; and enough has already been said on this theme to make detail unnecessary here.

An indirect effect, perhaps of equal seriousness, flows, not from the tool, but from its location. Industry is a town-process, and city life presents patent race-dangers. Rural birth-rates usually exceed city birth-rates, and city death-rates exceed rural death-rates, at least among homogenous and long-settled populations. Recent figures on occupational life-expectancy rate farmers highest and office-workers and clerks lowest; the average farmer lives to be fifty-eight years of age, the average office-worker to be thirty-six. Indoor vocations are more deadly than outdoor vocations; the average stonemason lives longer than the average machine operative. The English observed, fairly early in the industrial era which swelled old towns and built new ones, — Carlyle's "ant-hills," — that cities consume population. They put it long ago into a mathematical ratio sanctioned by common observation: fifty miles distant from London a family will last a hundred years; a hundred miles, two hundred years; the more easily a family gets to town, the more time it stays in town, and the quicker it disappears. Quick transportation no doubt has reduced the differentials in family death-rates by hastening the process of decay all round. Galton, proceeding statistically, found that London families run out in four generations; unless London were recruited constantly by new blood from the countryside, it would degenerate into a hamlet within a hundred years. Havelock Ellis, examining the biologic influence of London upon British genius, says of 1030 leading figures through seven hundred years: "It seems impossible to find any eminent person who belongs to London through all his grandparents. It very rarely occurs that even one grandparent was born in London." Great men and women were born in London, and great men and women were born in the country, of London-born grandparents; but within three generations eminence had departed from strictly city-bred lines. The evidence indicates that cities cause populations to degenerate in quality as well as to decrease in quantity. Of the two effects, the former, of course, is the more serious; quantity will usually take care of itself, while quality is something which must be either fought for or sought. That is to say, conflict, in a primitive society, enforces a standard of excellence automatically; while a civilization less brutal can achieve an equal standard of excellence only by taking thought for the morrow.

City life, with its hurry, noise, and confinements, puts the human organism under obvious strains. As Dr. Arnold L. Jacoby, psychiatrist of the Detroit Municipal Court, says, "City living uncovers weak spots in the mental armor, which might never have appeared under the calmer and less grinding condi-

tions of rural and village life." Certain races stand
the racket of the towns better than others. The Jews,
probably owing to immunity born of compulsory city
life through many generations, are biologically the
most successful city-dwellers; Negroes, a large proportion of whom are comparatively fresh from the
soil, the least successful. Anglo-Saxons, if London be
taken as an example, fare ill in towns. In general,
swart, short folk withstand congestion better than
fair-haired, long-geared peoples of the Nordic strain,
who seem to need space for their labors and adventure for their souls. In so far, then, as the Nordic
strains are esteemed superior contributors to the institutions we value most highly, industry has helped
to depreciate race-quality by concentrating machines
and men so thickly in cities.

Lothrop Stoddard puts the case squarely: "The
racial displacements induced by a changed economic
or social environment are, indeed, almost incalculable.
. . . . Two hundred years ago the Mediterranean
element in England was probably very small. The
industrial revolution reversed the selective process and
to-day the small, dark types in England increase notably in each generation. The swart cockney is a re-
surgence of the primitive Mediterranean stock. . . .
An ill-balanced faulty environment penalized the superior strains and favored inferior types."

And again: "The cramped factory and the crowded
city weeded out the big, blond Nordic with portentous
rapidity; whereas the little brunette Mediterranean,
in particular, adapted himself to the operative's bench

or the clerk's stool, prospered — and reproduced his kind."

In his "English Traits," written in the eighteen-forties, Emerson said: "The robust, rural Saxon degenerated in the mills to the Leicester stockinger, to the imbecile Manchester spinner, far on their way to be spiders and needles." Far likelier, the Saxon, broadly speaking, stayed on the land and sent his increase overseas (whole townships of my native county were cleared by such stalwart sons of England); while the human "spiders and needles" spawned from other and less sturdy strains, more amenable to discipline and less irked by routine. But, after all, it is less important to know precisely how industry causes depreciation in the British people than to realize (1) that England contains a smaller proportion of strong, beautiful, and independent beings than it did before Watt invented the steam-engine; and (2) that industry is in no small degree responsible for that depreciation in human values.

Striking evidence on this point appears in Philip Gibbs's "Now It Can Be Told." Two typical Englishmen fought the war. One was a cockney, small, nervous, nervy; the other, taller, more dogged, with more bottom for a long pull, revealing the traits long held characteristic of Englishmen. The latter predominated in country regiments, the former in city regiments. "The Bantams" did not represent the extreme decline of British manhood, but merely registered the decline down to a certain standard, below which throng still more unfit shoals of humanity, valueless in the supreme test of war. Below regulation height, but full of spirit, these Lilliputians tried their level best to play the man; but they could not walk fast enough, or carry pounds enough; and, after ordeal by battle, were taken out of the line and given less trying tasks. "Most of them" (says Gibbs) "came from Lancashire, Cheshire, Durham, and Glasgow, being the dwarfed children of industrial England and its mid-Victorian cruelties. Others were from London. . . . Some of them had big heads on small bodies, as if they suffered from water on the brain. . . . General Haldane, as commander of the 6th Corps, paraded them and poked his stick at the more wizened ones, the obviously unfit, the degenerates, and said at each prod, "'You can go — You — You.'"

General Haldane poked the Bantams with his stick and bade them begone. Whither? Whither, indeed, but back to their machines, where they belonged and from which they never should have been divided by duty. And there, to paraphrase the nursery rhyme, they function very well, better perhaps than the big fellows. At least, if not more efficient per man, they are no doubt more efficient per unit of output, else from such beginnings they would not have been produced in such numbers. Where the race was to the strong, they failed; but where the race is to him who turns out most goods at least cost, they hold their own and increase, if for no other reason than that they eat less. In a strictly utilitarian world, which ours may become if we don't watch out, to raise men taller than convenient machine-height may be esteemed a wanton waste of food-stuffs. Economic efficiency, in that case, would be attained at the price of physical deficiency.

Bantam body, too, may mean a bantam brain; in our section of America, where industry is new, but powerfully equipped with machinery admirably designed to oust mind from the common man's production, more than one leader close to the grind has told me that industrial efficiency, as carried on to-day, makes also for mental deficiency. One of my fellow citizens in charge of the industrial relations of a large factory shocked an audience of industry-adoring business men by saying, "We are putting the brand of industry — stupidity — upon the brows of our workers."

The tongue of the people speaketh much truth; twenty years ago we spoke of "the submerged tenth"; now, since the army tests showed that approximately one fifth of the registered adult males in the United States between 18 and 45 possessed mentalities below age fourteen, by test, we must speak of the "submerged fifth." And, lest it be argued that accumulating physical weakness and mental weakness in industrial countries are not incompatible with moral strength, let us recall that the average female delinquent now makes her first appearance before the police two years earlier than she did ten years ago. The average age of such appearance is now fourteen to fifteen years; it used to be sixteen to seventeen years.

Where and as functioning, machine industry and its accompanying urban congestion make survival easier for inferior strains and more difficult for superior strains. Genetic values, we are told, run constant; but automatic machinery tends, both directly and indirectly, to reduce the incentive for high genetic stocks to reproduce at former birth-rates, while increasing the incentive for rapid growth of low genetic stocks. Certain disgenic influences — such as poor housing, inadequate feeding, youthful excesses, lack of moral discipline, and an educational system not adjusted to compensate for the inhibitions of mechanized toil — may be overcome in the main; nevertheless, the tendency of our times is toward lower physical and mental levels for the led majority of the industrial group. There are offsets, of course, — notably higher standards of living for many families, and a growing power in labor to find leaders to bespeak its needs, — but as yet these are not potent enough to balance the scale.

We have been considering the effect of machinery upon normal folk; the parallel question of its effect upon the multiplication of defective mental types now presents itself. The highest type of mental defective, the moron, is defined by Pierce Bailey as "one capable of earning a living under favorable circumstances, but incapable of competing on even terms with his normal fellows." Below the moron status, this inability to compete becomes more and more marked; until, in the congenital idiot, it reaches the absolute. The idiot is either cared for or he starves.

This inability to compete for livelihood on equal terms exercised, from the very beginnings of human existence, a salutary check upon the multiplication of mental defectives. In the old days, when man competed nip-and-tuck against his fellows and the beasts, the less adaptable, slower thinking and moving members of the tribe were eliminated more speedily than we eliminate our weaklings. As long as skill remained the dominant element in winning subsistence, the less skilled were handicapped in finding wages, and so found it difficult to marry, support a home, and bring their young to maturity. Agriculture for the backward boys, domestic service for the backward girls — these were economic refuges for the inefficients. For those who could not meet the requirements of these occupations self-support was impossible. The Iron Man has now added simple routine factory work to the list.

The more simple and monotonous factory work became, the more advantageously the factory could use persons whose wits were neither keen enough nor elastic enough to master processes requiring skill and training. To acquire a hand-trade was beyond them; to use a simple machine judiciously, beyond most of them. However, as division of labor developed toward its present minuteness, higher-grade defectives were relieved to some extent of a burden under which their kind had labored from time immemorial. Automatic machinery gives countless men and women of low mentality economic opportunity, at wages approximately equal to those earned by higher types working at like jobs. Indeed, automatization has now reached a point where individual capacities of workmen count for so little that large employers of labor find less keen minds cheaper than keen minds in many berths, because the less keen mind presents fewer labor complications to the boss, is more easily satisfied, feels labor-strain less, and is less trouble all round. In other words, the intellectual level of labor fixed by the Iron Man is such that a moron trained in habits of doing, regularity, and obedience, is, for many practical purposes, more valuable to his boss for goods-production than one higher in the mental scale. Having brought to the machine less mental luggage of sorts not required by the shop, his adjustment to the present needs of industry is simpler for both parties to the labor-bargain.

This economic brace which the Iron Man gives to the defectives in their hitherto unequal struggle for existence translates itself to some extent into vital statistics. The twelve-year-old man (mentally) of grown stature, who works well in his machine-niche, may sustain a home and rear children in a security impossible to one of the same mental age a century ago. His wife may work in the mill, if she chooses; his children can get on the machines not long after the state gives them working papers. Since the low-grade man is always able to outbid and outbreed his betters, because content with a lower standard of living, the influence of automatic machinery and extreme division of labor is to drive higher mental types out of the shop, and draw lower mental types into the shop. This tendency battles at present against the shop's need to recruit foremen, superintendents, tool-makers, and other men of skill and leadership, to give point and direction to the routine labors of the mass of working folk; but this check may not long continue to be as important as it now seems, since manufacturers are beginning to look to public education to provide them with skilled mechanics, and presently may do likewise for foremen and superintendents. At any rate, since the thought-compartment of modern industry contains a minority of employees, and that minority tends to decrease in numbers relatively to the led majority, the pressure of the Iron Man biologically, at this stage, is toward descent-in-type. The few cannot lift the many biologically; the best they can do is to protect themselves against admixture through eugenic matings — a defense reaction laudable enough, but of extremely limited effect on the matings of the multitude.

Obviously, this view of the case leads one a step further along the path toward the pessimistic conclusion that industrial efficiency is forcing a cleavage between the masses and the classes, in mental as well as in financial and social status. We who live in factory towns know how steadily this gulf is widening; in spite of conscious and intelligent efforts put forth, it is becoming more and more difficult to establish and maintain social contacts between those who live on wages and those who live on salaries, rents, and dividends. The class-hired delegates to good works meet the border-line folk professionally, now that their principals have pretty much ceased to meet the masses socially; but uplift can scarcely be considered a social contact. Indeed, we seem well on our way to develop, with the help of the Iron Man and despite public education, an American proletariat, definitely shut off by mental lacks from the upper reaches of society — a considerable class numerically, whose contribution to the state is labor-time and children capable only of supplying more labor-time. The Romans named their lower class of freemen the proletariat, because its members proliferated freely, supplying the state with one essential to its life — soldiers. We seem by way of creating its duplicate, except that, in addition to supplying man-power for war, our proletariat may also be expected to do work for which the Romans depended upon their slaves.

This is a dire prospect, and a good deal is likely to happen to prevent it. But we must admit the tendency, and admit further that this tendency of modern industry to stabilize an ever-increasing body of deficients into a controlled servile class, to do our mean and monotonous work for us, draws strength from experiments in practical psychology. One such experiment, widely commented upon, was conducted by Elizabeth B. Bigelow, to determine the possibilities of subnormal girls in factory work. The field chosen was the production of rubber goods, in which process division of labor is less advanced than in many other lines of production, and hence presents more difficulties to the subjects up for training. Relating her experience in *Mental Hygiene* for April, 1921, she concludes that, with proper training, even those deficients previously discharged for cause can be trained to function efficiently.

"It is now generally known that the effectiveness of a mental defective depends less, within certain limits, upon the grade of mental defect, than upon the habits of doing that he has acquired. An individual with a mental age of eight years, who has definitely acquired habits of industry, obedience, and regularity, is a far more useful member of society than a high-grade moron who has never acquired such habits."

If industry is unwilling to take the expense of training defectives, Miss Bigelow thinks it would be well worth while for the state to pay the salary of a director. Both Miss Bigelow and Dr. Arnold Gesell, who comments on her report in the same issue of *Mental Hygiene*, commend vocational training for defectives in the public schools, in order to fit them for industrial work.

These and other investigators in the field of industrial psychology, in their zeal to render defective individuals self-supporting and bring forth the full productive power of the nation, may be overlooking some of the vital consequences of their programme. It is one thing to relieve society in this generation of the cost of maintaining a maladjusted moron or an institutionalized imbecile, and quite another to lower social tone and race-quality by enabling such, through economic adjustment, to count for more in the community and to rear more numerous offspring than he or she could as a derelict upon the ragged edge of existence. In practice, to make a moron's life more secure may be to make some more capable person's life less secure, if they chance to be competitors for the same job. In that case, you have change but no progress. Race and state, indeed, lose more than industry gains.

For the state to accelerate the progressive mental impairment of the race, by training defectives for industrial pursuits, seems to me the height of folly, unless, at the same time, it moves toward restraining the fecundity of those it places. Since a mental defective, on a machine job keyed to his powers, may be an industrial effective, his economic security is likely to work out in the normal directions of home and family. It may be feasible, as proposed, to control defectives industrially trained so closely outside of working hours that they do not propagate; but the dividing line between the normal and subnormal is so hazy that it seems unlikely society ever can restrain, by police power, the marital inclination of those just under the border-line. As long as a man keeps out of jail and meets his family responsibilities halfway well, the state scarcely can regulate the most intimate of his relations.

I have stated this problem of the biologic effect of automatic machinery to three psychiatrists. They agree that modern industrial conditions make for the perpetuation and increase of subnormal types. One voiced the opinion that border-line cases, through having more to offer economically, might secure better mates than their forbears, and so improve the strains. The others fell back upon the "servile class" theory. Briefly, that theory is this: since most of the work to be done in the world is of a monotonous, uninspiring sort, and more of it is coming to be done under conditions which strain painfully the average human of to-day, the development of a numerically large class of laborers, attuned to perform that labor at the least cost to themselves and society, is in the nature of an inevitable evolution. Highly sensible, thought one; while the other had his doubts. He considered it likely that the proletariat, after being leveled and debased by the Iron Man, might undertake to do so much leveling on its own account that civilization would be impossible.

To accept this theory of the servile class is to deny democracy, because the servile class could not govern itself. Whether those above that level governed ill or well, the result would not be democratic government, but aristocratic government. It is extremely doubtful if our people, possessing the ballot, will accept the logical working-out of current tendencies. They are far from ready, now, to accept without protest the decay of traditions of equality and opportunity, which, however weak in reality, are still dominant in thought. Therefore, the state, in order to preserve the present order, cannot let things slide to the point where the "have nots" accept solidarity as an accomplished fact. No matter what may be the temper of other nations under class alignments, the common American is not likely to acquiesce without argument in his being allotted a definitely servile status in society.

But whatever the state does to preserve its people from degeneration can scarcely become effective except after much turmoil, unless those who direct work-relations join with the state in combating the degenerating effects of automatic machinery. The enterprisers of modern industry may better afford to forego the economic advantage of hiring the least able-minded they can use, for the sake of maintaining an able-minded citizenry. Reason, after all, has its utility, not so much nowadays in mass-production, as in determining mass-action out of the shop — at the polls and in the streets.

Faced with a choice between docile, stupid labor and alert, less pliable labor, there is no doubt where the choice of the employer will fall who follows the economic motive strictly. Miss Bigelow says: "It is the quality of labor that has been given, rather than the intellectual level, that concerns the employer of this variety of labor." How far any employer follows that motive depends partly on competition, and partly on what he considers his duty as a citizen and leader. If pressed too hard by competitors, he may hold that he has no choice but to hire the cheapest, least troublesome individuals in the market for his routine jobs. But usually there is some room for the boss's ideals of serviceable citizenship to function in his business. An employer minded to make normal men fairly content on jobs in which defectives would consider themselves in clover, certainly could go a long way in that direction, provided the community and the state equally did their duty by giving the employed an inspiring social environment beyond the factory walls. To expect such an attitude from the leaders of American industry may be putting too much faith in human nature, as it grinds out goods and profits; but, after all, many of these men are great citizens as well as great manufacturers, and their sense of responsibility as citizens may reinforce their fear of social revolution sufficiently to move them to consider the intellectual level of their workers rather more than Miss Bigelow thinks.

Yet, when all is said and done, the utmost effort put forth against the degenerating influence of automatic machinery is likely to come, not from the state or the boss, but from those most injured by the multiplication of defectives — the workers in the shops. It is quite within the bounds of possibility that workers above moron grade will resent the introduction of defectives so keenly that bosses dare not make room in the mills for low mentalities as fast as they are produced. Even in unorganized shops negroes are now being kept off machines well within their mental range, because the settled public opinion of the shop draws the color-line. The employees simply refuse to associate themselves in toil with persons whom they hold to be inferior. Conceivably, labor may draw a mental line of exclusion as effectively as it now draws the color-line, and for the same reason — dislike to associate in toil with persons considered inferior and the desire to protect their jobs against such inroads. Insistence of craft-unions upon skill-requirements, even after machine-developments have vitiated those standards economically, draws a measure of social justification from this source — the standard so set protects the trade against mental as well as physical dilution.

The social necessity for more worker-coöperation in industrial processes finds one of its strongest arguments precisely here. If workers in unorganized shops at present can exercise a taboo against persons considered inferior by the working group, a kindred taboo against mental defectives will be effective in proportion as the workers gain cohesion and influence within the corporation. As group-pride rises, the stronger will be the protest against admitting to the group those who do not reach its standard of fitness, not merely for a particular job, but also for association in counsel and recreation. Here lies the most effective resistance industry can offer to the racial degeneration likely to follow upon the increasing industrial efficiency of mental defectives.

One swims even further into uncharted currents when one attempts to discover what the defectives themselves are likely to decide with relation to their own destinies. They lack normal initiative, and hence take kindly to direction and control; yet each continues to form judgments and act upon them as opportunity permits. What will be their attitude, for instance, toward birth-control? Their fecundity, to date, has resulted from necessity in which passion and ignorance join; pride of race and responsibility to the future certainly have not braced these slow-wit mothers for their ordeal. There is no reason for believing that the mentally defective woman wants more children than her abler sister; in fact, her attitude toward her infants indicates the contrary. If she knew how to avoid childbearing, the chances are that she would avoid that ordeal sedulously, simply because children are a bother, involving sacrifice and forethought, both of which attributes are in her most imperfectly developed. Notwithstanding laws against abortion, against the sale of contraceptive devices and drugs, and against the dissemination of information upon the subject, birth-control is a growing phenomenon. The state, whose continued existence requires children in quantity, has an excellent reason for continuing to outlaw the subject; nevertheless, birth-control is practised and gradually permeates lower and lower social strata. Along with syphilis and tuberculosis, abortion and contraception must be reckoned prime causes for the decline in the negro birth-rate in the United States in the last ten years. Twenty years ago there was talk of the negro eventually ousting the white race from America, through faster breeding; now the tables have turned, the white is winning the race, and the negro in America hardly more than holds his own from year to year.

Without attempting to draw any comparison between the average negro and the white moron as to mental capacity, I think we must agree that both are under certain disabilities predisposing them toward race-suicide. Neither possesses anything like social equality, or complete freedom of economic opportunity; both are under bans which may well lead adults to conclude that life is not greatly worth living for themselves, and presumably would not be valued by their descendants. When folk in that depressed state of mind know how to limit offspring, their women will dodge motherhood rather often, especially as home economic difficulties are equally eased by limiting the number of children born therein. Since defectives run greater risks than normals of death between birth and working age, it follows that any considerable decrease in births in families of low mentality might go a long way toward counteracting the biologic effects of their increased economic security in the Automatic Age.

Here, again, is a test of strength between economics and what may be called social education, the education of the times rather than of the schools. The schools do not teach birth-control, but the times unquestionably do; and if the most defective mentally are isolated in institutions, then those nearer the border-line may be held within bounds, themselves assisting.

Finally, a more stable balance in life and toil may be expected from this time on, a settling process, drawing strength from too many sources to permit of discussion here. At the moment this works grave hardship upon many wage-earners; but eventually it must inure to their benefit, as well as to that of the succeeding generations, since stability means rather more to the mass than flash opportunity. Emerson remarked, of England, that there is a temperance to be observed in making cloth, as in eating — a point worth noting and coming to be noted, never fear. To some extent, at least, overgrown industrial cities will be demobilized, and cities generally revert to their ancient status, as marts for the produce of adjacent territory. A folk nearer the land, and moving at a slower pace, may not press forward with such mighty leaps as we Americans have taken of late; but, so circumstanced, we shall be more firmly fixed and less affected by the degenerating tendencies of city living and mechanized toil, and have more time and opportunity to purge the body politic of poisons as they develop. Nature, the great physician, can help us there.

It remains to be seen how far our civilization, by forethought and decisive action, can overcome those declines in racial values which have unseated other civilizations and must destroy our own, unless checked. Civilization is a process in ameliorating life; and as life grows easier, weak strains in the population, previously kept under by hardships, increase in numbers. Machine industry accelerates the process, while science and altruism preserve to maturity weaklings who, under fiercer competition and harsher conditions, could never have lived to add their frailties to the stream of life. Gradually the weaklings accumulate in numbers, until the social structure disintegrates. Collapse, partial or entire, may follow war; in a rough world such is usually the case; but dry-rot within the walls is a standing invitation to the invader. Social revolution may be passive as well as active; peoples may have no will to defend the state, even though lacking initiative enough to change it through revolution. And until birth-control is world-wide there will always be potential invaders somewhere, waiting as waited Goth and Vandal beyond the Alps, for opportunity to inherit that which they could not build.

States come and go, for all their emphasis upon the

static; civilizations rise and fall; race remains and life continues. He who attempts to evaluate the effect upon race-evolution of these newer elements of life, — its modern tools and processes, — can do scarcely more than outline the problem, since we are here face to face with the eternal riddle of life itself. " One may say with confidence merely this and no more: the Automatic Age places the human family under bonds to posterity to use all its resources and wisdom in combating the degenerative tendencies of functional machinery in race-evolution. The battle for a better world may be won with the help of the Iron Man, but not through machines only; and not at all, unless reason replaces in large degree the captaincy which instinct now holds over industry and society.

X

EDUCATION FOR LEISURE

A YEAR ago I sat in a meeting of schoolmen and leading citizens, who were wrestling with plans for a new high school and technical college. The leading citizens were manufacturers of motor-cars, because our town's reason for existence is the production of such cars, of which we can be relied upon to deliver upwards of one hundred thousand a year, when the public buys them fast enough to clear the loading docks. Our leading citizens, consequently, are leaders in their industry as well. For downright public spirit, no more satisfactory group of employers can be found anywhere. They took it for granted that our new high school and technical college was to be keyed to utility. They wanted practical education, or, as one phrased it, "education for life." As their programme unfolded, it seemed that their goal was, rather, education for production. They may have seen new light since the wheels slowed down, but neither then nor later did the schoolmen offer any protest.

As an outsider, a member of neither group, I sat there dazed, silent, a little dashed and fearful, as one amid new ruins. I knew there was something wrong with the programme of these manufacturers; but what it was, I could not say. Now I know, because I have been studying the reactions of automatic machinery upon social relationships.

There is no better place for such a study than this town of ours. It exists for, and accepts the dictation of, industry highly automatized. In brisk times more than twenty thousand men and women work for three corporations, whose plants are full of automatic machinery. When these marvelous tools are busy, the town is prosperous, gains population, spends lavishly, yet saves much withal; when the tools are stilled, the town loses population, develops poverty, and lives on its savings.

In 1900 this was a quiet little manufacturing city of 13,000. In 1904 it produced its first motor-car, and growth from that time was rapid and sustained, draining away the surplus labor of near-by farms and villages. The 1910 census showed 38,550. In the next ten years, the city achieved a population of nearly 100,000, acquiring, among other interesting phenomena, a Little Poland, a Little Hungary, a Little Serbia, other immigrant colonies, and a Cosmopolitan Club financed by the Chamber of Commerce. We built a Polish church and school, two Russian churches, a Czech church, and presently we shall have a Jewish synagogue. During the war we imported camps of negroes direct from the Black Belt. All these non-natives, about 75,000 in the twenty years, came either to tend automatic machines, to supply the economic and domestic wants of the operatives, or to coöperate in a scheme of production in which the automatic tool was the decisive factor.

Of course, this growth induced the usual and to-be-expected rise in rents and land-values. We built houses as fast as we could find the money; but, in spite of enormous profits to constructors and investors, we could not provide housing fast enough to satisfy the industrial leaders. In 1919–20 the corporation controlling our two largest plants built thousands of homes. As a strike ensued, the builders fell back upon the principle which had profited them in automobile manufacture, substituting for skilled labor, machinery and unskilled labor.

In 1920, production on automatic machines here and elsewhere having outrun consumption, the wheels slowed down to a fraction of their former speed. Immediately our town began to lose population; thus proving that, with cities as with plants, quick growth means weak roots. Coincidentally rural districts began to gain. While we were losing 15,000 out of our 100,000, a village eighteen miles away added 20 per cent to its 1920 census of 400. Money brought these people into town, and, jobs failing, lack of money took them out again into the fields, woods, and villages. Michigan woods were full last winter (1920) of men who, the year before, were tending automatic machines. What back-to-the-land propaganda failed to do through twenty years, economic necessity accomplished in six months. The Pied Piper of modern times is the Iron Man, the automatic tool. Its staccato tune lures adults from their homes as inevitably as the Piper's tune drew the mediæval children of fable. To their ruin? Perhaps.

Of all the states, Michigan shows the greatest percentage of urban growth from 1910 to 1920. It also reveals the greatest growth in the use of automatic tools. This is because our state is the automobile state. An interesting study of the parallel development of the automatic tool and the automobile may be found in the June (1919) number of the *Journal of Political Economy*, under the title, "The American Automatic Tool." The author, Mr. E. F. Lloyd, shows that the automobile, as an economic want, burst into being rather than grew. It was a new means of transportation, not the development of an older means. Its makers faced the markets with open minds, and almost empty hands. They had no well-established shop-practice to consider, little or no machinery to junk. Their margins were large enough to ensure that whatever increased production would return profits. Moreover, the nature of their business required large outputs of identical parts, accurately machined, standardized, and interchangeable. Hence the automobile industry is to-day the most highly automatized. Hence the reactions of automatic machinery upon human nature and the social order may be observed here in all their vigor.

Those machines which tend to replace the worker, or reduce his function to a minimum, are described as automatic. They are so designed that the worker need not know the vital steps which the mechanism takes in producing the desired result. The dividing line between these tools and those that merely lengthen or strengthen the arm of man is nowhere definite and precise, but examples will help to point the distinction.

With the power wool-clipper, as with the sheep-shears, the mind of the operator must work with his muscle, to extract from use the increased efficiency of the tool. But with an automatic tool, the attendant is required only to feed the machine and relieve it of its produce from time to time. There are a good many semi-automatic machines; but the tendency is toward their complete automatization. Each year sees semi-automatic machines develop toward automatic perfection; each month sees the scope for skill in industry lessened, particularly in those basic industries which concentrate large numbers of workers in given centres, and so exercise a determining influence upon social relations.

Skill, of course, is still vital; but the need for skill has passed upward. Machine-design, shop-organization, routing of materials, and distribution of produce — these require a concentration of skill and technical knowledge far beyond the similar requirements of non-automatic industry. The rank and file need use only a fraction of their native intelligence and manual dexterity, while the skill-requirement, which formerly spread more or less over the whole shop, is distilled into a relatively small group of engineers and executives.

This shift of vital function from the man to the machine is the key to many problems. It affects all departments of life. We have seen how it broke down the barrier of apprenticeship which had sealed factories more or less against rural labor and brought raw farm boys into town, leveling farm and factory wages, lifting food-prices. We have seen the power of the Iron Man to pull the negro north and the peasants of Europe west. And we have seen something, but not all as yet, of his influence in shifting women from the home to the mill. The clear, unmistakable tendency of automatic machinery is to level labor, both as to supply and wage.

Certain collateral effects are equally impressive. Many automatic machines can be operated as well by a child of twelve as by his parents. In fact, the tender of automatic machines reaches his or her highest economic power early in life, when nerves are steadiest. The strain involved in nursing automatic machinery is a repetition-strain, complicated by clatter. The operative does the same thing over and over, amid rhythmic sounds, in an atmosphere frequently stale with oil or dust.

Youth stands this better than age, because youth reacts more quickly. Whereas, in the old days, a man used to come more slowly into earning power, reach his highest pay at thirty-odd, and continue fully competent until age began to slow him down at sixty-odd, his son leaps into high pay as a hobbledehoy, reaches his economic apogee short of twenty-five, and from thirty-five to forty-five slides swiftly downhill. He is a better earner at twenty than his father was; but the chances are that he will be a poorer provider at fifty.

I prefer not to be too dogmatic on this point. Automatic machinery is so new, having been in common use about twenty years and still being in its infancy, that present deductions on economic life-expectancy are founded upon too few instances to be altogether conclusive. Moreover, the swift decline of earning power in middle life may be partly due to causes only indirectly related to industry — poor housing, youthful excesses, and the like. However, present indications point to the correctness of the cycle outlined above.

Now the difficulties of the problem presented to educators by automatic machinery begin to emerge. The majority of youths, male and female, no longer need to be taught how to earn their living. Three days after the law that sets limits on child-labor leaves them free to work at the machines, they will be earning big money — practically as much as they will ever earn. There is little to learn; the mills can teach that better and cheaper than the schools.

The pockets of these children are full of money at an age when their fathers earned less than a living wage as apprentices. They are economically independent of home and social control. They have the eternal belief of youth, that the preceding generation is fossilized, and the buying power to act upon their belief. They are foot-loose to go wherever automatic machines are turning. They can buy their pleasures, and they do. They can afford to flout age and authority; they do. Their very active minds have no background, and feel the need of none. They have no conception of the cost of civilization; no standard of reference by which to judge social and political questions. They have not even lived long enough to learn the simple truth, that common sense and wisdom spring from the same root. With far greater need for early thrift than their elders, because their effective economic life may be shorter, they spurn the homely virtue of economy. They buy pleasures, buy companions, buy "glad" raiment; they try — desperately — to buy happiness. And fail.

Yet they are splendid raw material for citizens. Let a great cause kindle them, and they rise to it like knights and ladies — *noblesse oblige*. They met every war need more than halfway; fought and fell; sacrificed and saved — during the emergency. Their faults are those of youth, *plus* affluence.

Here is the explanation of our youthful delinquency. Our "bad men" of this winter are mostly minors. "My court," said a Detroit judge, "is the scene of a procession of beardless boys." They acquire appetites, expensive appetites; pleasure leads into bad company. A prank gone wrong, an unfortunate slip, a month without a job and nothing laid by — and we have the beginning of what we call the crime wave.

All this, of course, is more marked in brisk times than in dull times, but even in dull times youths so employed earn as much as older men; and, lacking the domestic responsibilities of the latter, are able to flourish independently of their parents and devote to youthful pleasures a buying power roughly equal to that of adults.

Much as this situation complicates the educational problem, the school system somehow must be adapted to it. Somehow these children must be brought up to a mental and moral level approximating the economic level upon which they set foot immediately after leaving school. This is a grim task. In the public schools, certain things must be taught before the age of sixteen, which now are taught only in college, and to which many college students appear to be immune. The proposal itself would be revolutionary if it did not arise from a new set of industrial conditions, to which society is accommodating itself clumsily, but, in the main, peaceably. As such, the change, though startling, is clearly evolutionary — and inevitable.

What are the positive educational requirements of the machine age? To clear the ground, let us eliminate the non-essentials. The child who is going to tend an automatic machine does not need, in any economic sense, to read more than a shop poster or direction sheet. If he can sign his name to a pay check, that is enough. If he is willing to trust the shop to figure out his pay, he need not know his numbers. For the time he stands beside the machine, his earning capacity is not increased by anything he knows. Knowledge may be useful in getting him away from the machine, but that escape is going to be more difficult as automatization proceeds toward its logical conclusion. Such knowledge as the operative comes by in school possesses for him only a cultural value. It does not help him in the least to earn his living; but it helps him immensely to spend his leisure.

For these children — these prosperous, precocious children — possess leisure, and the means to make the worst of it. They work, most of them at least, no more than eight hours a day. Presently, it may be seven, even six. As production becomes more and more automatic, the wants of men can be supplied with less and less labor. Consumption, of course, may expand enormously; yet the demand for goods remains ever in stiff competition with the universal demand for leisure. " I.'ve got enough; let's go fishing," was a state of mind so common in 1919 that it disturbed factory schedules, roused employers, and set tongues wagging about labor-profiteering.

Employers may fight the tendency toward the shorter working-day, but theirs is a losing fight. For a time, in our town, we went along, producing on a five-hour schedule all of our kind of automobiles that the restricted market would absorb. Every day was a half-holiday for thousands. More recently hours were lengthened, and the number of days of work per week decreased. If a factory operative got in more than three days' productive work in the week, he was lucky. Saturday has been a workless day in one of our great plants all winter. We have discovered that with picked men, heightened morale, and a closer synchronizing of all the elements involved, production per man can be greatly increased, even doubled. If the present highly effective organizations are slowly enlarged, thus preserving their efficiency, it is difficult to see how the market, under normal conditions, can absorb more than eight hours' produce from day to day.

If this seems to contradict previous observations on the elimination of the personal element through machine use, please note that the improvement is due largely, if not altogether, to the work done by the engineers and executives in more efficiently routing materials to the machines. Under boom conditions,

the stream of supply was often interrupted, thus
throwing the machines out of production. This has
been largely corrected; also, in the meantime, the
machines have been tuned up, and new ones added in
some cases. The attendant of the automatic machine
remains just where he was; but the machine has the
chance to do more and better work. Of course, even
in a highly automatized plant, there remain a good
many jobs that require either no machinery or semi-
automatic machines, and in such cases the recent
weeding-out of the ineffectives does produce beneficial
results. If the market will not absorb the products of
the longer working-day, on the present more efficient
per-man per-hour basis, then it seems apparent that,
viewing the country as a whole, industry will have to
adjust itself to eight hours or fewer, probably fewer.
The nation's supply of automatic tools is not going to
be decreased simply to lengthen the working-day; on
the contrary, competition continually forces more and
more of such tools into operation.

A shorter working-day manifestly means greater
leisure for the masses. Whether the free time comes
from choice or necessity, from labor-bargains or lay-
offs, that free time is none the less leisure. Now it
is everlastingly true that the bulk of human mischief
is done in spare time. There is precious little chance
for original sin, or any other kind of sin, to work itself out under the strict regimen of a modern factory.
While human beings are at work, they are, perforce,
reasonably decent. The employer sees to it that the
time he buys is not wasted; but no one exercises an

equal degree of control and supervision over a man's unbought time, — his leisure, — unless it is the man himself.

In a town dominated by automatic machinery, therefore, the educational problem is to train youth for the right use of leisure. Why waste time teaching city children how to work, when their chief need is to know how to live?

Precisely here is the point of my argument. Education for leisure, under the conditions of automatic production, is education for life. The attendant of automatic tools does not live while he is on the job; he exists, against the time when he can begin to live, which is when he leaves the shop. His task does not call for a fraction of his full powers as a sentient being, or monopolize his interest. If he could buy the same amount of well-financed leisure as easily in any other way, he would shift jobs to-morrow. It is impossible for him to grow mentally through his work. So he comes to his post as a slave to the galley, and leaves it with the gladness of a convict escaping prison. Psychologists say that a large part of industrial unrest is due to the inhibition which automatic tools place upon the expression of personality through labor. Be that as it may, the fact is, that the hours given to tending automatic machines are given to buy leisure; and in that leisure the operative lives. He lives in his sports, at the movies, at the prize-fights, at the blind pig, as well as at the theatre, the lecture, the library, in the park, and on the front porch of his inamorata.

In general, it has ever been true that leisure is the

cream of life. We have tried desperately to build up
an immunity to leisure, with our dull gospel of work
for work's sake. There is a glory in creative work; but
even that becomes pain and weariness if we are kept
too long at it. All labor produces, sooner or later,
weariness and pain, nature's signal to quit and go
a-playing. When does that most stolid of men, the
peasant, live most fully — when he plods the endless
furrow, or when, at evening, he sings his songs, dances,
prays, and courts his maiden? When did the skilled
mechanic of another day feel his manhood soar highest
above clod and worm — when he was chasing a screw
with a cold chisel, or when he was taking the air in his
garden, or, perchance, hobnobbing with his mates in
the corner saloon? Is the tireless business man better
company when he is chasing a golf-ball or when he is
chasing a profit? Is the banker best satisfied with himself when he is figuring interest or when he is hip-deep
in the stream, figuring trout? I think that men of the
better sort reach their furthest north in life, not in
the hours they pay for life, but in the hours they spend
in living. Certain am I that none but an imbecile
could find much delight in sharing the daily toil of our
mill-workers, so mechanized has it become. Consequently, education for leisure is precisely education
for life; and education for life comes down, squarely
down, to education for culture.

To apply the early Victorian ideal of education to a
machine age, to call upon Matthew Arnold to pre-
scribe for a flurried and worried democracy, may seem
absurd. But that is what the situation needs; and the

necessary is never absurd. That cultural ideal was to fit for leisure those who had leisure — a small minority. With certain reservations in the interests of truth, it may be said to have produced a few first-rate minds and a very considerable number of gentlemen and gentlewomen. Now, because leisure has broadened out to include the majority, we must cultivate gentlemen and gentlewomen *en masse*. What was once a privilege for an arrogant aristocracy has become a necessity for an arrogant democracy. Unless our American gentlemen and gentlewomen appear in due time and in sufficient numbers, civilization will be wrecked by machine-made barbarians, unable — though their machines compass the globe — to replace what they have destroyed.

What is the first requirement for the right use of leisure? Self-restraint. Leisure is liberty from an exacting, definite control — that of the boss. In leisure a man is subject only to the state. When the worker leaves the shop, he passes from a positive control to a negative control. Inside, he is required to do certain things; failure to do them results in sure discovery. Outside he is required not to do certain things; although, if he does them, no penalty may follow. Thus we see that it is immensely more difficult to train human beings for life and leisure than for toil; and that in America only odd and unusual persons get very much out of leisure. About all that a retired business man feels equal to is golf and musical comedy. The workers offer more encouragement — Brashear and Henry George showed what laboring men could do in spare time.

Need for self-restraint increases in direct proportion
to leisure and affluence. Temptations to break the
law beat upon the impecunious idle; but temptations
of another sort, scarcely less subversive to character,
beset the idle youth with money in his pocket. I am sure
that eight dollars a day at eighteen — and some of
our lads earned much more than that — would have
corrupted me beyond repair. The wonder is, not
that some of these highly paid striplings go wrong,
but that all do not do so, considering the opportunity offered them by their cynical and predacious
predecessors. More even than wild oats, I am sure
that such buying power early in life would have insulated me against right relationship with the world
of ideas and ideals, past, present, and future, by blast-
ing nascent inquiry and speculation.

The establishing of this relationship in youth is, I
take it, the end of all true and worth-while education,
involving as it does the subjugating of the assertive,
unbaked Ego to the social well-being, as manifested
in the legal, moral, and ethical codes prevalent in one's
environment, and enforced, more or less, by the power
with which common consent invests political institutions. Respect for authority, even that qualified as-
sent involved in the pragmatic view of established
institutions, has extreme difficulty in getting a root-
hold in a generation whose youth is economically self-
sufficient.

It follows that knowledge, as the chief restraining
influence in the youthful mind, is the substitute that
education must establish in place of the set of controls

which formerly resulted from the young man's poverty, or fear of poverty. Remembering that the rising generation reaches its highest economic utility early in life, and that it soon, relatively speaking, reaches the economic status of old age, I think we must agree that, unless youth is taught thrift, pauperism will lengthen and strengthen from this point in time. A grievous outlook, to be forestalled at any cost.

There is need, therefore, to drill thrift into children; let the experts busy themselves on methods. The whole field of economics must be opened earlier, and charted more simply. Is it not odd, in a nation that bows down to economic fact, to find that the teaching of economic theory is almost wholly a college monopoly? It ought to be possible to begin the teaching of economics in the kindergarten, and to bring the pupil along so that, before he becomes a part of the economic machine that supplies human wants, he may understand at least its delicate nature. Suppose a child of five were set to moving by hand a given number of blocks, from this space to that — an hour's work. Then suppose the child were given a basket to ease the job — time, ten minutes. Then, suppose further that an intelligent teacher explained that the basket wascapital, the result of previous thrift, of labor in past time. That lesson would stick. Somehow to get this, and other fundamentals, into the mind when it is plastic, is the supreme educational task of the future.

So with the idea of law. My children know, among other surprising things, the chief products of every state in the Union; but they have no conception of the legal system which enforces equity and fair play in the exchange of those products. It seems the simplest thing in the world to teach them that laws exist to protect the weak from the strong, the just from the unjust, the person of good intent from the swindler. Once they had mastered that idea, they might see the policeman as a friend rather than as an enemy, and our economic-juridical system as something to be protected instead of destroyed. A generation so reared might insist upon the law doing its primal duty; but it would be evolutionary, not revolutionary, in its demands.

But self-restraint is not, of course, all that a man needs in order to make something out of leisure. A man may be ever so self-restrained, and yet be desperately bored at the prospect of spending an hour in his own company. Self-restraint is merely the brake upon the ego-motor; it will keep the individual from running amok in society, but it will not start anything. Its virtue is negative. What the ego-motor needs in leisure is fuel, something upon which it can travel, progress, journey into new realms of thought. The best fuel for the purpose is compounded of interest in the present, understanding of the past, and sympathy with the future. History, literature, science, art, music — all these give to life meaning, and to leisure, inspiration; a reasonable concern in all that man has done, is doing, or is about to do upon this planet — with such equipment any fool could use leisure aright. To sow that seed is the first duty of educators, now as always, now more than ever.

So much for the background. But backgrounds are always hazy; let us concentrate. Since work is coming to be no longer a primary interest for the child of the masses in civilized lands, it is incumbent upon us to provide, in so far as they can be provided, other primary interests through which the individual can justify his existence, interests which, rising out of, and sustained by, his background, shall flourish like the green bay tree all the days of his life. Every man, whether he works a turret lathe or a comptometer, needs a hobby to busy himself with, in this age of growing leisure. We hear less of vocational training than we did — for good reason, since its utility is passing. Presently we shall hear more of avocational training, which shall give every youth destined for the mill or office a hobby for the centre of his garden of leisure.

In a machine age the applied sciences are paramount. Let them remain so. There are important posts on the peaks of industry which must be filled. Let us see to it that every mind fit to join the directorate of industry gets its educational opportunity. Machinery is undeniably one of the prime intellectual interests of the American masses; in leisure an informed generation would continue inventing, perhaps invent faster than ever. Therefore let us give youth all it can stomach of the sciences, deepened and broadened to the uttermost. But by no means should we submit to the specialist's obsession, that, with the key to universal knowledge in his hand, he travels down a walled alley, shut off from the humanities, from philosophy, from religion, from life.

I am not competent to provide the synthesis for this analysis, to describe the educational reforms which are necessary, and which, I am sure, are on the way. That is a task for many and mature minds. But certain key-points emerge out of the haze. We must, I think, insist upon ten years' schooling for every child, as an irreducible minimum, before plunging into the whirl of automatic production. There should be four school terms instead of two, with a brief holiday between; the long summer vacation is an anachronism in a factory town. So also is the Saturday holiday — six days a week in school henceforth. There is so much to be taught, and there are so few years to teach it in, that youth must hurry. At the same time, school should be so much more interesting, that the charge of drudgery could not hold.

Then, too, there must be more teachers, and smaller classes; better equipment, more money spent all round. Finally, there should be a complete system of continuation schools, wherein those who desire to use their labor-bought leisure by securing further instruction, could be accommodated on their own time. All graduates presumably will have been so far inoculated with the intellectual virus that they will go on improving their minds in leisure to some extent, thus demonstrating on a wide scale that education is not a matter of youth, but of life. With such a start, the many will read, discuss, and enjoy the noblest works of man. And some among them, have no fear, will create as well as recreate.

But the programme, after all, may be left safely to

the specialists, now that the problem is stated for their attention. They may have been a bit tardy in seeing how the Iron Man is frustrating their efforts, and why; but that is because they have been concentrating upon an even more wonderful mechanism — the human mind. Let them quarrel, as no doubt they will, over the details of the programme; but they can be trusted to accept the statement, — once they square the facts by the rule of reason, — that the welfare of our people and the preservation of our institutions depend upon our educating youth to use reasonably and gloriously the growing leisure which the common use of automatic machinery has in store for humanity.

XI

GOD AND MAN

THREE innovations in a single notable year so affected the development of modern Western civilization, that the new world may be considered as born in 1776, when Adam Smith published his "Inquiry into the Wealth of Nations," the American colonies revolted from Great Britain, and Wilkinson made Watt's steam-engine a commercial success by boring cylinders capable of holding compression.

The effects of the first two are tritely acknowledged. Smith's logic broke down the so-called mercantile system of state control, freed trade from many of its political inhibitions and opened the door to individualism and commercial opportunity. Here, on our eastern seaboard, the search for freedom, renewed under favoring circumstances in a rich environment, resulted in a representative government amenable to democratic ideals — a consummation so appealing to men, that the political trend thereafter in all enlightened lands has been away from personal power and toward constitutionalism, away from feudalism and toward democracy.

Not the least important of those three great adventures was that in tool-making. Until Wilkinson perfected his boring machine so that cylinders could be produced true "to the thickness of a thin sheet of paper," Watt's engine remained merely an interesting and ineffective model. But no sooner could steam-engines be produced in numbers, than Watt's contribution became a mighty force, not only in fabricating and transporting goods, but also in fabricating and transporting civilization. Hard, indeed, to find a man or institution on this planet not in some way affected, for better or worse, by the steam-engine and the industrial civilization built on that base. Even the Sacred Lama of Tibet has seen an Englishman, a camera, a repeating rifle, and a dotted line upon which to sign away some of his sovereign powers to inheritors of the steam-engine. The applied science of Watt and Wilkinson has been as revolutionary in its effects as the politics of Jefferson and the economics of Adam Smith.

No event of first-rate importance since 1776 can be explained satisfactorily without reference to the three forces then released. The trio have pulled in harness, and while one might at some point seem to be carrying most of the load at any given time, the fact is, that all three were in the news every day, though often unrecognized. To discern where the paramount influence of one ends and that of another begins calls for more application than is worth while, since the workings of each have been qualified by the others, and the three together propel modern Western civilization.

These three — politics, economics, and science, in their modern manifestations as democracy, competition, and the harnessing of natural forces through mechanics and chemistry — have brought vast boons and vast sorrows. They have given us tubes under London and trenches in Flanders, the ocean liner and the submarine, motor-cars and depth-bombs, laugh-

ing gas and poison gas. They have enriched life abundantly and destroyed it ruthlessly, letting poor folks
have luxuries that kings could not enjoy of old, doub-
ling the population of the earth in four generations,
and killing, maiming, and starving some 40,000,000
in four years. They have given us means to more
material prosperity than our higher natures can as-
similate, lifting the standard of living without lifting
equally the standard of conduct. The soul of man
wanders dismally among his marvelous machines, trying to salvage the tattered bits of his ideals, and piece
them together into chains strong enough to bind again
the greedy beast he knows his lower self to be. Still
searching! Thank God for that!

This is a tragic time. With small heart for the task,
we are mopping up after a debacle. We take our wages
grudgingly. Even the least of us seems to be aware
that we shall fail if no vision comes to us; even the
hardest pressed knows that cash in hand, be it large
or small, is not enough to nerve the soul of man for
victory over himself. Having won a victory over Nature, and turned the spoils of that victory against
himself in his madness, Man now contends for victory
over himself. If he fails, his civilization must perish
in a morass of materialism, where men contend for
wealth and power as swine at the trough. In that
case, we shall have created our own barbarians, and
our spectacular civilization will deserve engulfment
in another Dark Age.

Each golden age in history has had its dénouement
in which fair promises come to wreck upon the points

of unseen rocks whose bases are primordial human traits. There is that in human nature which checks our species short of realizing the dreams of its noblest sons. In part, the reason is economic; alas, we must eat and be clothed, and contend for the privilege of living. And yet these difficulties are not insuperable, considering the enormous productivity of our modern tools and processes. Primarily the failure is due to the fact that each generation must be schooled anew in restraint, while the instincts, and likewise the tools and processes that lend themselves so readily to the gratification of those instincts, are inherited intact and vigorous. The apparent weakening of the religious, moral, and ethical controls since the Industrial Revolution began may be relative rather than actual. Those controls may be stronger than they were, and yet, so much more intense are the material forces against which they must contend, the controls seem relatively too weak to hold.

If 1776 be considered the beginning of an epoch in which politics, economics, and science increased their influence steadily, and at a constantly accelerated pace, over human affairs, then 1918 may be considered a halfway point in the great historic cycle. Not merely the other side of a circle, because history is a whorl; the figure, if you please, is one in solids, and the plane of the beginning impossible to regain. But, at least, the trend henceforth, for many years to come, must be back toward the beginnings. One would be blind, indeed, to miss the accumulating evidence that the human spirit, weary of what men have done — for the most part unwittingly — by and through politics, economics, and science, looks back despairingly from new to old. The Prodigal, reeking of the fleshpots, turns toward home.

After much experience with democracy, we are forced to qualify democracy. The "free and equal" clause of the Declaration of Independence is a dead issue, no longer valid among us either practically or theoretically. We are forced to recognize inequality as inherent in human nature, and accept class-distinctions as having psychologic as well as economic bases. Opportunity to climb from one class to another or to sink from one class to another, is as close an approach as this generation can honestly make to professions of equality. No matter how thoroughly the progress of automatic machinery levels wages, or how incomes are leveled by super-taxes, ability and intellect will herd together and lead. We perceive that the hope of the world lies in the exalted leadership of an aristocracy recruited from all classes of society on the basis of merit; and that, while the common sense of the masses may be trusted in fundamental decisions, the complications of civilization are such as to make the mass-verdict of value only on simple issues where ample time is available. So far have the theories of democracy been qualified by the wisdom of experience.

Likewise, the evolution of our times proceeds relentlessly, despite terrific opposition, toward a revival of mercantilism through state control of business. "Do as you please as long as you pay your taxes" is as dead as that ultimate of *laissez-faire* economy —

free trade. Individualism took too large a dose of its own medicine, and fades day by day. The tradition of personal independence dies hard; yet die it must when confronted with the reality of personal interdependence. We rely upon the state and the community to preserve the amenities of social life against the ultimate effects of economic pressure. Coalescence of individuals into groups has progressed so far that coöperation is essential to the civilization we know. In the extension of the coöperative principle resides our best hope of industrial peace, and yet confidence enough to make coöperation work is lacking and must be rebuilt. Our world is full of social controls unknown to our forefathers; but an older world than theirs knew something like them in the far-away days when individual initiative was hampered by the state at many points, and the church, as a sub-government, touched all lives.

The analogy of "return" may be pushed even further. Our corporate groupings take on more and more the look of feudal groupings. Insecurity in toil and station has made good its curses as well as its blessings. Labor searches for security as well as for reward; and the renewal of labor's confidence in the capitalist system seems likely to await the success of efforts being put forth to harmonize security with freedom — a task desperately difficult, perhaps insuperable.

In all these respects, and many others, a disillusioned world seems to be retracing its steps toward a point where life was simpler and more easily reduced to rule. It is a weary round, because we moderns, in the meantime, have come by so much disconcerting knowledge and have had so little time to reduce it to comprehension. Mountains of facts weigh us down, and we have no æons of time at our disposal, to let natural forces work these facts into strata of gold and dross, easily recognizable for what they are worth. Many things appear important to us which probably are not important at all, but seem so because we have lost our old standards of selection and appraisal, and lack new ones whose validity is commonly accepted. In the press, for instance, enough energy and material is wasted girding at women's clothes to go some little distance toward implanting economic sense and social ideals in the minds of the people. A noisy evangelist, by circus methods, stirs thousands of weak minds to acknowledge a Master they forget next month. A captain of industry is advertised into mythical hero-ship by an energetic press-agent, and the country thinks it has discovered someone worth while. These are vain things; fortunately time will blot them out, and history contain no record of them, except perhaps in satire. Nevertheless, they keep us from sane judgments. Our minds are open channels, through which ideas rush without finding lodgment or stiffening into convictions.

Difficult, too, to keep the plane of return an ascending plane. How much easier it is to let industry degrade the masses, than to give them a leg up through coöperation, and a hand up through cultural education. Easier to accept the moral code of a given moment as sacrosanct, and strive for a lifeless morality through law, than to examine that code, bring it down to date, and educe goodness through suasion. Simpler also, to accept cold formalism in religion, than to seek for the spirit behind the forms, or to strive for a new definition of the Deity acceptable to generations steeped in Darwinism. Why bother with trying to bargain ourselves into a *modus vivendi* which shall compass both social welfare and individual growth, when we can have the whole dreary round soon over by rushing pell-mell into state socialism and risking the consequences? Now, as ever in such heartaches, men are sorely tempted to try short cuts. The highway following the folds of nature is long and flinty, and our feet are bleeding. Yet short cuts, now as ever, end in quicksand.

If I knew of other controls than religion, morality, and ethics, for the ills of materialism that beset the workaday world, the temptation to present them in this conclusion would be too great to withstand. I have made bold to point out, with appropriate reservations, certain sedatives; but I repeat that there is no panacea short of revising our whole attitude of life toward wealth production and distribution. That, I am satisfied, is impossible: the instincts toward possession and dominance are too strong. The best we can do is to strengthen where faint, and renew where absent, those ancient religious controls which brace men for duty, justice, and mercy.

No one knows better than I the insufficiency of saying, at this pass, "Morals" to the mass, "Ethics"

to the class, and "Religion" to all and sundry, meanwhile pushing briskly by on the other side of the road.
Morals, we have been told too often, are matters of
convenience and custom, latitude and longitude.
Ethics, unless reduced to code, are too hazy for guidance, and, when codified, are soon outworn in this
changing scene. Both morals and ethics may be at-
tainted as born of expediency, except where they
spring unbidden to the surface in a character fertilized
by religion.

A self-made banker put the case neatly: "Ethics!"
he said brusquely; "I know how to spell the word; no
more. Yet I am reputed an ethical banker, in a day
when opportunities to make tainted money safely in
my business are many. What keeps me from taking
them? No fine-spun ethical notions, I assure you.
Simply old-fashioned religion, learned in an old-fashioned home."

One heard in the boom days much talk of service
and ethics, and many protestations of business morals,
at luncheon clubs and the like; but these did not hin-
der business men from canceling contracts right and
left when prices were fluctuating rapidly, and thus
contributing to a destruction of confidence which is
certain to afflict the trading and working world for
years to come. Even business honor, the ethics of
counting-room and market-place, needs a firmer base
than expediency. In the most materialistic concerns
of life, practical men have been surprised to discover
that the spirit animating the disposition of resources
is of prime importance. Bricks, we are relearning to

our sorrow, do not make a wall unless the bond between them holds fast against ill winds.

We moderns suffocate under an avalanche of facts; our distress is due, not to the facts, but to our difficulty in discovering their relationships, and reducing them to comprehensible order. Our age, more than any other, is oppressed by a necessity to reckon with relations between things and ideas; we understand with growing clearness that in life all is intertwined. That which gives the infinite concerns and phenomena of life meaning is the bond holding them together. Civilization is a synthetic process, a truth which those who have been trying to save it by analysis and specialized thought do not seem in the least to appreciate.

The most durable bond that Man has yet succeeded in discovering is belief in God. The fact that one can write indefinitely long of industry and make no mention of God may be at the root of more of our industrial and social troubles than we imagine. Adam Smith saw no future for the corporation except in a few lines easily routinized, such as life-insurance. Little did he foresee that inventions would so increase the routinizing apparatus available for use by compelling personalities, that the corporation would become in our day the established form under which business proceeds. Equally, we give no sign of comprehending that human beings are routinized along with business. Something infinitely precious evaporates from the soul of man in the desert of routine. The idea of God has less and less chance to express itself in the worklife of the common man, as chance is crowded out of his toil. For God is the essence of freedom; He alone has the freedom of omnipotence; and when work is mechanized to the point where outside, uncharted forces cannot affect production, God is reduced from a partner to an onlooker.

I refuse to add another unsatisfactory definition of God to all those on record. An extensive theological library (inherited) shows me the folly of that. Let who will declare God a person or a force. I have never had a mystical experience of God, and find myself unable to subscribe with a whole heart to any creed I have ever read. I know not whether God is one, or three, or a thousand. The Invisible King of Mr. Wells is as unsatisfactory to me, and no more so, than the Jahveh of Joshua. It is not my province to find a Deity acceptable to the modern world; but rather to point, unwillingly and from laggard conviction of necessity, that it is high time for us moderns to quit considering our systems and machines as all-important, and to search for God with what strength is left in us.

There was a time when I subscribed to the anthropomorphic conception of God: that man made God in his own image — an extended and glorified image, to be sure, but essentially man, multiplied in goodly personal power and shorn of the baser traits of humanity. For all I know to the contrary, that may be the case; but if Man did invent God, I hold that invention to be the masterpiece of human wisdom, far outstripping in usefulness any and all subsequent innovations of the "brave, little biped." That, if so, was the first step in progress from beasthood toward manhood, the essential without which self-restraint and social order are impossible. With God, however discovered, in the saddle, Man was ready to march, as he could not otherwise have marched, toward the command of all things terrestial. Assuredly he could not have come so far without God; and unless he keeps his faith in God, this present quagmire is a turning-point in the journey, and "Retreat" the order of to-morrow.

I have come to this conclusion from inner compulsion, after viewing the evidence, and against the protests of some, more sage than I, who hold that Darwin and his successors ruined the concept of God past repair. If so, then the scientists planted the seeds of ruin in our industrial civilization even as they built it, because industrial civilization cannot hold together unless the idea of God as Universal Father and All-wise Judge increasingly restrains the follies, greeds, hates, and ambitions of men.

There is pathos in a trade-paper tale out of India, wherein Hindu steel-workers are described as decking their machines with garlands on holy days, as once they decked their bullocks and their ploughs. We smile indulgently; what pleasant, simple children, so likely to be cheated in a game in which we are grown stale! And yet that naïve reaction to machine-power is no more absurd, and rather more picturesque, than our organized efforts to bring God into machine-shops through welfare work. And its very spontaneity is in refreshing contrast to our penchant for the mechanized, departmentalized activities of the modern institutional church, fit refuge for standardized souls, and as near like a factory as ever a church can be.

The masses remain incurably mystic, but to-day their mysticism moves them less toward organized religion than toward social revolt. How much of the machine-tender's unrest is due to the feeling that he is forsaken of God in his toil, no one can say. He is sick, I think, of working for bread alone. The success of the A. Nash Company, with its Golden-Rule policy, indicates that men relish being considered, not as numbers in a card-index and as companions of machines, but as members of a fellowship founded upon common consent of God and common descent from God. Kneeling together, praying together, and singing hymns together may be all very well, but, if no religion can be injected into working together, then God has been crowded out of the most influential phase of modern life, and the confident continuance of the wages-system awaits His return.

Assuredly many of us are daily doing God's work, as the statesmen tried to do it at Versailles, without daring to assert their conviction of its acceptability to Him. We are grown strangely reticent on religion, and strangely immodest on personalities. We are forever chattering about the big men in industry; but if one of these forceful beings should say, "This I do to the glory of God," we should hold him a blasphemer. Yet such thoughts, no doubt, inspire men to unselfish action even yet; and, if avowed, might be understood by those who cannot stomach, at this pass, pretensions to moral and ethical elevation.

The religion of toil, if one may dare a division of religion for the sake of emphasis, is neither ecstatic on the one hand nor formalized on the other, but quiet, unpretentious, and vocal through deeds rather than words. And where breaking into words, seldom do the words convey a tithe of the full meaning behind them. On certain massive stone arches, at the borders of two industrial cities in New York State, are graven these words: "The Square Deal Towns: Erected by the employees of the Endicott-Johnson Company." They bear the likenesses in bas-relief of two men. I should like to know more of those men, and get at the reasons why they inspired those unique community memorials. If all is as it appears, then those arches seem to me more significant than the Arc de Triomphe, or any other marker of victory. Indeed, they evidence a more unusual victory, — the triumph of mutual service in toil, — and are as honorable memorials to the thousands who erected them as to the two commemorated thereon. The builders might have added, "To the Glory of God"; but there is no need: the phrase speaks in the work; for where men work in faith and confidence one for another, there God manifests Himself unceasingly. And until that faith and confidence return, God shall be sore needed in industry.

Politics, economics, and science — these sustain and order life; but the life they offer is too barren of spiritual satisfaction to give joy in and of itself; too harsh to hold the loyalty of those who fail to win its high prizes of cash and place; and too complicated for ordinary folk to reduce to inner harmony, unless they take much on faith and have in God a unifying concept.

The duel is on between that culture of the active soul which democracy offers as a final value of life and a mechanization of mundane affairs so complete that democracy as we know it must perish under its sway. Our successors shall not come out of this conflict spiritually victorious unless they are sustained by faith that their labors are acceptable of God.

Further evolution of automatic machinery may cancel from the equation difficulties which now seem important. Fatigue may depart from industrial toil as machines become more and more perfect. But even so, an adjustment between human interests and machine interests must still be made somewhere — if not in the shop, then in the streets, homes and legislatures. As machines come to do more of the necessary work of the world, the right use of leisure as an antidote for sloth and luxuriousness and as a means of mental, moral, and physical health becomes essential to national vigor. Likewise, as human beings become increasingly dependent upon machines for the means of life, who shall own those machines and how shall their produce be divided ? In escaping from one sort of travail, man runs straightway into another.

Consequently, whatever the trend and pace of evolution, Man will have need of Divine assistance toward wisdom and patience in order to emerge strong and serene from the struggle with the Iron Man.

Seaver-Howland Press, Boston.